WRITING FOR
YOUR READER

WRITING FOR YOUR READER

Dick Friedrich

Angela Harris
Forest Park Community College

KENDALL/HUNT PUBLISHING COMPANY
2460 Kerper Boulevard, Dubuque, Iowa 52001

Printed in the United States of America

B 402157 01

This book is dedicated to
Larry, Lisa, Julie, and Ursula Friedrich
and
Mary, Tom, Cindy, and Don McCallen
and also to
John and Louise Harris

There are no answers in the back of the book.
Soren Kierkegaard

Everyone is in the best seat.
John Cage

Preface I

Ten years.

It's a whole decade since David Kuester and I began work on a text eventually to be known as *It's Mine*. A couple of years after we started it, it was finished with the editorial consultants Greg Cowan and Liz McPherson doing much more that I would have expected. It would be only a slight exaggeration to call them co-authors. And now I'm the only one of the four left in education: David and Greg are both dead and Liz has retired from Forest Park Community College—the place where we thrived for most of those ten years.

Now, much has changed—not merely the name of the year. Teaching has changed, teaching English has changed. The students this year are different from the students of ten years ago—not better, not worse. Just different. They have other reasons for going to school; the teachers have different goals for teaching. We all know the details.

But the book has changed too, surprisingly enough—in odd sorts of ways. When we finished it and sent it off to our publisher, it was perfect—it was the book we wanted it to be. By the time we read the first copies sent to us by the publisher, we saw some changes that needed to be made. And the longer we had the book in our hands, the more classes we taught with it, the more material we saw that needed changing. We received over a thousand letters from students who had read the book, teachers who had used it and critics who reviewed it. It was gratifying that virtually all of these pieces were warm and laudatory. And it was helpful to read their suggestions. Hopefully, we learned as the decade passed.

Enter Kendall/Hunt. They asked me if I had thought about doing an update of *It's Mine*. No. I hadn't, but I had thought a lot about re-doing it. Kendall/Hunt, it turns out, would be interested in such a project. I went to Angela Harris who agreed to co-author a new book and so here it is.

The journal is still a central feature; the activities are still aimed to give students specific experiences which they should synthesize (with the guidance of the teacher) into concepts about how writing can communicate most effectively, how they can use writing to share their most important thoughts; this book also stresses the importance of details and development of ideas for the reader; it still stresses the importance of the reader to the writer. The activities have been considerably simplified; nevertheless, they remain centered on the students' experience and ideas—as opposed to having the students write about matters primarily of concern to the teacher.

There are, however, major differences between this book and its predecessor. The whole journal has been done by Angela; she has focused on the usefulness of the journal in this book to students who will be keeping their own. (The journal here does retain the novel-like characteristics of the previous journal—in fact, as our students find out, most journals do end up telling a story.)

The book itself (journal and text) is less flamboyant. While we have tried to retain legitimate playfulness where it seems entertaining and useful, we have tried to do away with what looks today like show-boating. The tone of this book is generally more calm than *It's Mine*. Related to this change is that this book is a good deal less dogmatic. The longer I teach (over two decades of college teaching now) the more sure I am that this approach to writing is a valid one. Interestingly, the more sure I am of what I do and the way I do it, the less interested I am in wasting my time convincing others to think likewise. This major shift has made this book a good deal less shrill than its parent.

I feel, finally, that the main strength of this book is that it treats writing as more than a silly if difficult skill to be mastered. I have for years been convinced—and I am more so now—that the continuing perfection of our writing is an important human activity: one that justifies itself. Writing to and for a reader remains for me one of the most important activities we carry on as human beings.

What remains fundamental to me is that, as humans, we are still lost, we are still doomed, we are still alone. This is part of our condition. On the other side of this scale (but not quite balancing the gloomier side) are our moments of community, those moments when we reach out to share our feelings, our ideas, our lives—in short our selves. These moments, I believe, do not merely keep us from madness or make our existence merely bearable. Rather they make our existence momentarily sensible. We may still be lost and doomed, but—for the moment—we are no longer so ridiculously alone. If it is silly to fall for this illusion, if our minds force us back to awe-full reality; never mind. Because we have transcended. For those moments 1 have ordered myself and my universe. And (to paraphrase Faulkner) I have not merely endured. I have prevailed.

This is the context I write from. I intend for this context to give perspective to this book.

Dick Friedrich

Preface II

Here are a few bits of advice that might come in handy for people—students and teachers alike—who find themselves using this book.

Students should read the book through during the first month of the semester. This is so that they can have a general sense of what the purpose of the book is before they study the chapters individually. Moreover, having read the journal sections of the book, students who are unfamiliar with journal keeping will have a model. We suggest that students also reread the whole book toward the end of the semester in order to tie together what may seem to be disparate concepts.

While it is not necessary to require students using this book to keep a journal, this particular kind of writing works very well with this book. Teachers can handle the journal in a number of different ways: some teachers require 7–10 hours of writing per week from each student and read only those parts of the journals which students may ask them to read; other teachers require fewer hours of writing each week and read everything; still others require a certain number of entries, perhaps 3 or 4, each week. These journals can be collected each week, once a month, or whenever the individual students choose to turn in their writing. Teachers may read the journals without comment, or comment with or without including consideration of grammar, mechanics, and spelling. Journal entries can be used as bases for revised papers to be used as class assignments or may be the major writing assignment of the class.

Conceptually, the book can be divided into three parts: fundamental aspects of language, the need for adequate detail, and the writer's consideration for and analysis of his or her audience. It considers the nature of language; more specifically, how language is used in communication; and most specifically, how language functions in written communication.

We don't think that it is necessary to try to do all the activities suggested; it may, in fact, be impossible to do them all during a semester. But we do encourage everyone who uses the book to write more than is called for in the suggested assignments because it is only by writing that we can, after all, learn to write.

Angela Harris

Acknowledgments

We would like to thank Sheila Harris who designed the figure used at the beginning of each activity section in the book and in the cover design.

. . .

We would like to thank Liz McPherson for her long time friendship and encouragement. And to tell her that we miss her.

AUGUST 28

Today is the first day of the semester. I'll be
keeping a journal of one class throughout the
semester and, with any luck, will learn something
from it. Since, obviously, this journal is also for
you, the readers of this book, it will be a bit more
selective than a journal that I keep for myself
alone. The specific topic for this journal will be
one class that I am teaching, my 8:30 Monday and
Wednesday evening first semester comp course. I do,
however, reserve the right to write about anything
else that seems interesting, relevant, or just plain
there. (I should explain that I am easily amused and
have an almost senile fascination for minutiae so
that every now and again I launch into discussions
about essentially boring things.) Please bear with
me. One of the things that's nice about a journal is
that the writer can be as self-indulgent as he or
she wishes. I'll try not to get too carried away,
because in spite of what I believe in my heart, my
head tells me quite clearly that nobody else is
really interested in the fact I wore Happy Hiker
saddle oxfords instead of Spauldings like everyone
else in my high school.
All of this is by way of introduction of the
journal, and of me. Though why I feel the need to do
the latter, I don't know. I suppose it's that in any
piece of writing, you create a world. And
understanding that you, as a person writing, are the
shaper of that world makes writing a very self-
conscious activity. You are, after all, telling what
you know, to an audience you pick, in a manner you
choose.

AUGUST 28

It is now 11:30 at night. I have met my class
for the first time. I did not tell them about this
journal because it would have made me nervous to

admit it and because if it doesn't pan out I, the
writing teacher, would have to admit that I didn't
keep a journal while I'm requiring the members of
the class to do it themselves.

I explained the general requirements of the
course this evening, answered a few questions, and
laid out some groundrules for the class. I've become
a very strict enforcer of the no smoking rule since
I'm planning to live another 60 years and I won't
make it if my lungs encounter too much pollution;
but I am in favor of eating: I think that anyone who
attends a class that begins at 8:30 at night should
be encouraged to bring along a snack or something to
drink if that makes late night learning more
bearable.

The students seemed generally receptive to my
regulations, if, in fact, they can be called that.

I am now going to treat myself to a chocolate
covered cherry, watch Kojak, and go to bed.

AUGUST 30

Tonight, I asked the students to introduce
themselves to each other. It's always interesting to
me to hear what people say about themselves when
given this task. Feminist literature has pointed out
that in our culture a man, introducing himself, will
talk about his work, and a woman will tell you who
she's married to. I'm not sure how consistently this
holds true, but it is an interesting exercise to
listen to what people have to say about themselves
given just a few minutes.

Having the introductions occur in a class
directs many people to introduce themselves in terms
of why they are in the course. One woman named Carol
explained that she was an RN and wanted to get a
B.S. in nursing so she was back in school for her
''academic'' courses. Several people mentioned job
advancement as their reason for being in school. A
number of the students made it clear that they'd

been out of school for awhile and were a bit nervous about returning.

A number of other things were mentioned too. One man, Willy, said that he has always wanted to be a pro-football player and a small red-headed woman told us that she was financing her education with money she had earned publishing her own book of inspirational poems.

I always feel a lot better about a class when I can individualize the students—when I know who's who and have some sense of where they come from. It seems that the students feel much the same way.

Chapter I

"Hi there." "How's it going?" "I love you." "What this country needs is courageous, imaginative, and responsible leadership." These look like words, don't they? We can look them up in the dictionary and find out what they mean. And when we use them we know that our listener will understand. So we use them and talk and write and live and die with our mouths and pens constantly moving. Using words.

It seems simple enough. A word means something: that is, it contains some meaning. If I talk or write those words, everybody will (or should) understand. We learn a few when we're very little. Then we get to be about five or six and we go to school and our teacher teaches us a bunch more, in addition to showing us what the words look like when they're put into writing. We move on through the grades till we reach college. There we hear a lot more words and we learn them. We're really on our way to being intelligent.

We take tests. The more words we know the better we do on them. The better we do on them, the smarter we are told we are. An occasional good grade and an occasional bad grade on themes in English goad us into trying to learn more fancy words and how to use them. By this time words are almost as much a part of us as our fingernails.

For now let's stop to see what this important part of us really looks like. How does it fit into my life? Which language is the best? The most difficult? If English is the most difficult, does that make English-speaking people smarter than other people? If we taught English to them, would they become just as smart as we are?

First, the notion of words: what is a word, really? Take a look at the following passage:

Early this morning, as I stood in the libstil, I thought "I wonder what makes a person want to become a binneck? Is it the herob? I doubt it. Is it fun to plem? Maybe. At any rate I sure never want to be a binneck."

Later, after I had been pleg duwe, Mary came smid and said, "George offered me ten lidden if I would herob to become a binneck." I burrew for a sned and sned and said, "you bask lud rassel."

Look at that passage. Those strange looking words. Are they words? Do words have to mean something? To whom? What if they mean something to me, but not to you? If they mean something to seven people, but not to the rest of humanity? Is it a matter of majority rule?

 (1) Try this with the passage and the "words" for which you have no "meaning": Write a meaning for each word in this list so that the passage makes some kind of sense to you.

libstil_____

binneck_____

herob_____

plem_____

pleg_____

duwe_____

smid_____

lidden_____

herob_____

burrew_____

sned_____

bask_____

lud_____

rassel_____

O.K., everybody has a meaning for them. Now are they words? Maybe it would help if everybody had the same meaning. **(2) So decide as a group which set of meanings you want to adopt. Use the following alphabetized list to make a small dictionary of agreed on meanings.**

bask_____

binneck_____

burrew_____

2

duwe_____

herob_____

libstil_____

lidden_____

lud_____

pleg_____

plem_____

rassel_____

smid_____

sned_____

Once you're satisfied with the words, use them. Write your own stories using the words, and read them every day to each other for a couple of days.

You probably will discover after using the words for a short while, that you know them as well as you know "regular" words.

(3) Discuss the meanings of the following terms:

foreign language

bad, or dirty language

correct or wrong language

bad grammar

bad spelling

SEPTEMBER 6

When I first told the class about the journal requirement, I did not give very specific directions about what could be in a journal. That's because I think that someone who is starting to keep a journal has to explore subjects on his or her own. One result of this is that the first entries in the journals my students turn in often include questions and some confusion.

3

Here are several entries from the class's
journals which were turned in yesterday. Ralph
Williams started his journal this way:

So this the first day of beginning my
journal. I'm not too sure about what exactly I'm
suppose to be writing about. But if this is to
be a daily journal about everyday life I should
be able to write something. For instance as
usual I was fifteen minutes late for work. I
guess thats because late last night about 1:30
a.m. I got a long distance phone call from a
friend in Atlanta, Ga. Now its time to begin
work. I am a custodian for the board of
education at Walnut Park School. Its a
elementary school that only goes to the fourth
grade. My job isn't really hard it consist of
the usual custodial duties, but its always
something different happening with the children
around. Of course its different right now
because the teachers are on strike. So really
its nothing to do right now but to sit and talk
the other custodians Wes, Jim and then my best
friend the matron Mrs. Howard. We always have
something to talk about. Its really just like
working with family. There are times when I
really enjoy working with them. For instance
today I had to change a light bulb in the boys
gym, which really isn't hard, but I'm afraid of
using the ladder. After trying for about fifteen
minutes to get the globe off, I completed the
task. So that will do it for the morning chores
for me. Probably after lunch I'll do some more
work. The good thing about the strike is I get a
chance to do homework done. I still find myself
nervous about attending Forest Park because its
been almost ten years since I was in school.
Just getting use to the routine of study and
work. There are times when I become nervous
reciting or reading in class. But as time goes
on I guess I'll get over it. I really enjoyed
the English Comp class last night. Some of the

stories were really good, I even felt pretty good about my own story. Even though, I thought it was a bit corny, but at least interesting. I wished I could enjoy my algebra class. Because I seriously believe I'll have to withdraw from class, if I don't catch on soon. I'll hate to fail a class on my first try back into school. You know its hard to write four hours a day. I've been writing for two hours and it seems like six hours. And whats worse is this is written in pencil, and I might have to copy this over in pen. That should be alot of fun, along with the rest of my homework. You know I taking twelve class hours. Now I've just about run out of things to write about. Unless you want to hear about my private life as well. There's really nothing to tell. I'm twenty-eight years old and single. I have one son thirteen years old who's now living with his mother in Atlanta, Georgia. I kept him with me until this past December. I felt it was quite a big responsibility for my mother to take care of him since my father died in August.

This is the first entry from Willy Theiss's journal:

Well here I am starting off my first day of homework in my first day of college in my entire life . . . . This project may be a little hard for me. I've been doing absolutely nothing that even looks like homework or schoolwork since my Senior year of High School. I can't believe that it's been 11 years since I sat in a class room and actually did any school work. I guess I'll catch on in a little while though. . . . I started this <u>abortion</u> called higher learning (or whatever) just for the money but it looks like I may start to like it. Already I've written almost 3 pages and I'm not even warmed up yet.

I took down the past two classes and took some
of the comments from the tape.

''The last time I heard somebody talking like
this, they took him off to the home.''

''When does English start?''

''We're trying to get some order into this
chaos.''

''You figure out what a word means by all the
words you hear around it.''

''This must be what the Tower of Babel was
like.''

''You want to use my definition, or have you got
something that's better?''

''I've got a bigger vocabulary now, but nobody
understands me outside of group two.''

''There's no way to resolve this. What's a
binneck for me isn't a binneck for you.''

''Ms. Harris, he won't accept my definitions,''

''Do we get any credit for this, or what?''

''Does the majority rule here?''

''Group one makes that word sound dirty.''

''Can you make a word mean something there's no
word for in English?''

''Wait just a damn snid.''

''The snidmen were some of the best fighters
there were then.''

''You know, after you've used these words a few
times, you don't have to stop and think about them
any more.''

''The test that group one wrote is racially
discriminatory.''

''Where do words come from, anyway?''

''Are you trying to teach us how to think?''

''That's his definition, not mine.''

I've been sitting here re-reading those comments from class and racking my brain for some profound observation to make about the whole thing. My brain isn't supplying me with much in the way of insight but that may be because I've got the television turned on to a re-run of <u>The Six Million Dollar Man</u>.

Last spring I vacationed in Los Angeles and during a tour of Universal City saw a demonstration of how the great feats of Steve Austin, the Six Million Dollar Man himself, were created. But it's still magic for me. Perhaps that's why I'm not having deep thoughts. The fact that we humans can communicate at all is magic to me. I know a bit about the physiology of producing speech, I understand that language is an arbitrary, symbolic system. I talk a lot, I write some, I read all the time, but I still think that communication is magic.

I'm reminded of an essay about language that David Kuester, another English teacher wrote. Let me include an excerpt from that piece.

In some primitive religions there was the idea that the word had the powers of the thing itself. If you uttered the word in a certain way, you could be hurting the thing itself. It must have been a frightening and intimidating world to have to live in. But at least, even if words sometimes had a kind of magic attached to them, they had power. The connection between the symbol and the thing itself wasn't viewed as merely arbitrary, but as integral, and if it was a petty and vengeful god who punished you for mentioning his name, at least he was concerned and active in human lives.

When we view the kind of arbitrary connections that do exist between words and things, and when we develop this kind of nonmagical, almost scientific detachment, I wonder if we weren't better off ''primitive.''

Now the events of time and space and the universe are arbitrary; our wishes have nothing to do with them.

God, if he exists, doesn't respond to the uttering of his name by one of us, even with a bolt of lightning.

And so we are alone, our words but empty, arbitrary shells that we are to an extent stuck with, but stuck with only because lots of others are stuck with them, too, and not because the word ''god,'' for example, by any stretch of the imagination, sounds like whatever entity that word might, in reality, or even in our imaginations, refer to.

We are left with loneliness and a language that is inadequate to make communication possible across the barriers of loneliness. We operate with a few words, uttering them repetitiously, and the private world of the person to whom we are talking is not our private world, and the words have quite different meanings for him, it turns out, and we are more alone than ever, screaming out in our inadequate language so that it may, in its volume, if nothing else, express our loneliness and overcome it and make it possible for us to speak to other human beings and be understood.

Reality is not simple, and, if language is too simple for reality, all we can do for the time being is take that into account and, maybe, begin to work to change that a little.

SEPTEMBER 18

Over the weekend, Dick and I and four other friends, Bev and Mike and Liz and Kaye drove down to Alton, Missouri, close to the Arkansas border for a canoe float on the Eleven Point River. The river flows through the Mark Twain National Forest and we planned to float along a section called the Irish

Wilderness. Our three day jaunt was to include floating Friday afternoon, camping out Friday night, floating Saturday, camping out Saturday night, and floating Sunday morning.

We had heard a lot about the beauty of the area and were pretty excited about the adventure. Five of us had gone sailing together for a week last year in British Columbia and figured we could handle anything. Well, we couldn't, exactly.

As Don, the owner of the canoe rental place, was helping us put our boats in the water, he mentioned casually that there had been a flash flood the preceding week during which the river rose nine feet. ''But,'' he said, ''it's okay now.'' He wasn't quite right. The river had gone down again but there were still some spots where the water was both fast and deep (unusual on Missouri rivers) and there were many logs and trees that had fallen into the water, reducing access and causing odd currents. We, however, were undaunted—for forty-five minutes.

We decided to camp early and cook steaks. Bev and Mike pulled their canoe onto shore, Dick and I followed with ours, but Liz and Kaye didn't make the turn they needed against the current. Next thing I knew, Liz was shouting to us that Kaye had fallen out of their canoe. Bev and Mike pushed off the bank to help. Kaye was by that time standing in the water about four and a half feet deep and had tied up their canoe to a tree. Bev and Mike tried to pull into a natural inlet but found themselves slammed up against a fallen tree with water swamping their canoe. For one foolish moment, Dick and I thought we could help them. The same current that swamped them, swamped us. I fell out of the canoe as we tried to avoid hitting Bev and Mike. As I bobbed up in the water, which was over my head, I heard Mike say, ''Dick's under the canoe.'' I thought he meant our canoe which was capsized and breaking loose so I went after it to save him. (I should mention here that I am a weak swimmer and am afraid of water—why I go sailing and conoeing is another issue altogether.) In just a few seconds, the canoe had

sped past me and I was in water over my head
realizing that while I'd love to save Dick, I had a
more immediate problem: saving myself.

My good instincts said ''float on your back,''
but the water was fast, I was weighted down with
shoes and socks, jeans, and a sweat shirt (my sister
who had lent me the shirt told me later that she had
been swept down the Colorado River wearing it), and
so, I went under again. At the time of this
particular submersion, I cursed the fact that I was
dressed as I was and that I wasn't a good swimmer,
and that I'd been dumb enough to go on the trip
anyway. Moreover, I told myself sternly that I did
not want to die. I bobbed up out of the water again,
shouted ''Help'',—something I never do until I'm
really in trouble—and went under again. The third
time I came up, I heard Dick shouting, ''Float on
your back, I'm coming.'' This time I did manage to
get up on the water and float, but I must have
realized immediately that I needed to do something
more since I was still being swept downstream. I saw
a tree overhanging the water about ten feet closer
to the river bank and up ahead, so with a
combination of floating and swimming, and one spot
where my feet touched bottom, I got myself to the
side and grabbed the tree.

Dick discovered me hanging from the tree and
called out to find out if I was all right. Hearing
my ''yes,'' he set off after the canoe which was, by
then, headed independently to God-knows-where. Dick
eventually caught up with the canoe which was caught
under another log and after rescuing as much of our
gear as he could, sat on the log sunning himself dry
in the middle of the river. He had to wait for us to
come find him because he had lost his glasses in his
first plunge and couldn't see far enough to know
what, if anything, the log he was sitting on was
attached to.

After about two hours of fighting water, hauling
what gear we had salvaged, and securing the canoes
which we could not pull up out of the water, we made
camp. We were left with one canoe afloat, one three-

person tent for six people, five dry sleeping bags,
dry clothes for everyone but Kaye who had lost her
clothes bag and couldn't fit into anybody else's
clothes, wine, beer, and food but no hard liquor
which we all wanted by then, and no cooking
utensils. We made a fire and cooked our hotdogs on
sticks while we tried not to think of the steaks we
couldn't cook.

After a night of cozy, but not very sound sleep,
we set out on foot to find a road carrying oranges,
grapefruit, nuts, and water and a few clothes. For
seven hours, we climbed over river bluffs and Ozark
foothills, ignoring the fact that we were in
Copperhead country and that we really didn't know
where we were. After about six hours of hiking, we
found a beercan (I know it's trite) and not long
after found a road and an old man in a car. From
there on in it was easy.

* * *

When I told Dick that I had written about the
float trip, he showed me a letter he had just
written to his niece describing the same
misadventure. After I read his version, I decided to
include it here with mine. After all, one of the
things we're both trying to say in this book is that
writing comes from an individual's personal style
and perception of an event. There may be many rules
about ways to write, but unless a person knows what
he or she has seen and wants to say, the rules are
about as good as grass seed on a freeway.

So here's what Dick wrote to his niece Mary:

As for me, Angela and I went on a float trip
last weekend. Left Friday and came back Sunday—
went to Alton Missouri—the Eleven Point River—
just this side of Arkansas. A float trip (if you
don't know about such) is when you load up a
canoe with food and sleeping bags and tents and
like that and paddle thru scenic territory. So
Angela and Me and four others (one being Liz

11

whom you know who was here for a few days
vacation) put in enough food for six weeks,
sleeping bags, two tents, cooking equipment and
changes of clothes and pushed off. We foated
(that is to say flaol—goddam it floated, now
thaz got it—I don't think I'll make it as a
typer) for about 45 minutes till Bev and Mike
swamped. Angela and I ran into them and turned
completely over. Kaye had just fallen out of her
canoe and Liz was the only one left inside a
canoe. I was under water coming up under fallen
trees and the upturned canoe. Mike said—Dick's
under the canoe. And Angela thought he meant our
canoe—when it was actually Bev and Mike's. Our
canoe was beginning it's independent float, so
Angela grabbed at it and went off with it to get
me out from under it. Me in the meantime was
having this chat with myself under water—relax
and look up for an opening and now swim up. So I
did. I got up out of the water in time to see
this blue form fall off the floating away canoe
(it was Angela, but I couldn't tell except by
deduction that it was her cause my glasses were
in permanent residence at the bottom of the
river) So I started paying attention to our free
spirited canoe and chased it about a quarter of
a mile. It got stuck on its own under some
fallen trees. So I fought some of our stuff out
of it and layed them up on the log and got swept
under the log a couple of times which gave me
the experience of swimming against the current,
about 3-4 minutes to make a yard back to the
tree. Hard swimming, by the way. So we salvaged
what we could and got ourselves back together.
One 6x6 tent for us to sleep in—sardine city. We
had all our food—steaks etc. and nothing to cook
it in. We got a fire going and ate hot dogs
cooked on sticks. Tasted good, too. Then the
next morning we went off thru the woods carrying
nuts and berries and water and some clothes
walking back to wherever we thought we might
make it to. After six or seven hours walking we

hit a dirt road with an old man in a car, who
took us back to the world. Sunday, I went back
up river with this guy who worked at the boat
place and we retrieved it all—except, of course
the stuff we had absolutely lost. And did I
sleep sunday night? (correct answer: yes) you
betcha me I did.

So here I am back safe etc etc and looking
forward to replacing the stuff I lost and
getting back out onto a river again and not
screwing up again. By god.

Some obvious differences between Dick's letter
and my piece have to do with the specific
information included and the amount of attention
given that information. There are several reasons
for this: I devoted much more space to my own
solitary adventure down stream a) because that's
what I knew about—I couldn't see what was happening
to everyone else; and b) ultimately, the most
important thing to me was my near drowning and
rescue.

You'll notice that neither Dick nor I had much
to say about Liz and Kaye's original mishap: we
didn't see it; even afterwards neither Liz nor Kaye
could explain how Kaye ended up in the river; and it
was important to us only as the event which
precipitated the chain of disasters. We mentioned
Bev and Mike only insofar as they affected our
actions too.

Dick and I had similar purposes for writing. We
were both telling what we saw and what affected us
on the float trip. I was also trying to reveal
something about myself to the readers of this
journal, who, at this point, know little about me
and Dick was talking to his niece, who already knows
him well. My audience was a group of comp students
who would be reading at some future time, and Dick's
audience was his niece, Mary, who would be reading
his letter in just a few days, so, of course, we
needed to explain different things.

Even though Dick and I wrote about an experience we shared, our pieces were different because we are different people who saw different parts of the event with our own particular insights and wrote about our experience for different audiences.

Chapter II

My grandpa's living room had its own smell. When I was a little boy and he held me in his lap, he'd smoke one of his fifteen to twenty daily cigars and drink a bottle of beer. More often than not, he'd be eating an onion too. After many years of cigars, beer, and onions, these smells blend together with his brown leather armchair to symbolize for me my grandpa.

Most people wouldn't like the smell, but I did. He sat in his brown leather armchair with me on his lap and breathed on me and gave me a sip of beer and a bite of heavily salted onion and told me stories of Bertie Haas, Naperville, Illinois' contribution to big league baseball. He'd tell me stories about my Dad and uncles fighting with the tough kids across the street.

Most of the time, though, he'd teach me to draw. Boxes and trees, birds and elephants. (I never did master them.) We'd sit there all Sunday afternoon and draw and we'd celebrate when I'd get all the lines right on the box: Grandpa would go into the dining room and bring back the pink glass candy dish with candy corn in it.

Once, on Christmas, I ate a whole dish full of candy corn right after a big family dinner. When Grandpa came into the living room to start drawing boxes and trees, he saw me lying down with a very pale face.

"I don't feel too good, Grandpa."

"Do you have to throw up?"

"No, I don't think . . ." At this point, it all came up on Grandpa, Dick, and the living room rug.

I remember being ashamed and embarrassed—uncles, aunts, and (worst of all) younger cousins saw me in the midst of my vomit. But Grandpa cleaned the whole mess up without noticing anybody but me. He put his arm around me and patted my back and calmed me down. "It's all right, Dick. I do it myself. Did just last week. Ask Grandma." Then he put his favorite bathrobe on me, the wool one with brown and tan vertical stripes.

Then he went down to the basement and brought up some of his home-made wine—to settle my stomach. Maybe he knew a lot about drawing birds and boxes, but he had no idea of how to settle a kid's stomach. I finished about half the glass before I threw up whatever was left after the first time.

Greater shame.

But all Grandpa did was clean up again and wrap me up in his brown leather armchair. Now, you have to understand about that chair. It was

Grandpa's. By that I don't mean simply that he owned it. It was his. Nobody else ever sat there. It wasn't that he ever told anybody not to; it's just that nobody ever thought of sitting there. But he put me in it and there I was, sitting alone in Grandpa's chair with him kneeling beside me wiping my forehead telling me all was well until I fell asleep.

Grandpa's been dead for nearly twenty years now. But when things don't go right with the world and I sit in my own brown leather armchair, I can smell him and hear him and feel him near—or, more precisely, the whole complex of feelings of security, warmth, kindness, and patience comes back.

Now let's say I want you to understand this part of me, to share it, to know what it meant to me. If I said "brown leather armchair" or "candy corn," or just drew a tree, you wouldn't get it unless you had shared the experiences connected with these objects. That's pretty unlikely; I'd have to tell you all the things that happened between me and Grandpa—something I can't do, because I've forgotten most of them and, even if I did remember, you wouldn't sit still for all the stories. So what I do is either tell you a few of the important events and hope you'll get the idea or else try to find music or colors or lines or words which hopefully would stir the same feelings in you.

But no matter which way I'd choose to communicate—music, colors, or words—I'd never be sure that you got the point. We could talk for hours discussing the attempt and our reactions and perhaps we'd even be satisfied that communication had happened, but we'd never be certain.

Here's an example to demonstrate the difficulty in more concrete terms. I like pigs. I used to take care of them on a farm. I found them to be loving and intelligent and pretty. I remember my favorite; she accidently got bred too young, so young in fact that she was unable to feed her babies successfully. One by one they died; with each death her head hung a little lower and she became a little more lethargic. I shall never forget when the last one died. She went over to the body and whined; she shoved her snout under the body in a futile attempt to get the baby back on its feet. She did this for over an hour before giving up.

On the other hand are chickens. If a mistake was made in the making of the world, it was surely in the creation of chickens. Their hygiene and thus their smell are disgusting. It isn't an honest dirt smell like that of pigs; it's a sour disgusting smell. They are also vicious; just put a wounded hen into the henhouse with her friends—it won't be long before they have pecked her to death.

Now let's say I am trying to explain to somebody what my feelings are toward my daughter, Ursula. I say "She's a little pig." Or "She's like a chicken." My listener probably wouldn't get the chicken idea. And it's nearly certain s/he wouldn't get the pig line. That is, s/he might catch on that saying she's like a chicken isn't a compliment; s/he surely wouldn't understand that calling her a pig is a loving statement.

I'd have to explain that one is a compliment and the other is an insult; perhaps I could even refine the distinction by talking about pigs and chickens and my experiences with them. But I'd never know for sure that he knew exactly the complex of notions that go into "pig" and "chicken" for me. And this might be the biggest challenge a writer has. I struggle constantly—as does anyone who writes—to give my readers the idea I have, knowing that they are going to bring ideas with them. For example, I might have a clear idea of what I mean by "a friendly person." Because it's so clear to me what I mean, I'm tempted to say that "everybody knows what a friendly person is," and let it go at that. Well, everybody does know what a friendly person is—but everybody knows it differently. As a result, if I don't explain or illustrate what I mean, my readers will understand the phrase based on their own definitions instead of mine and I will not communicate.

 Now it's your turn to write. Take an object that means a great deal to you and write about it so that a classmate will understand that that object has special significance. Don't let yourself say anything like "My ink pen is important to me because . . ." Communicate by showing the experiences that went into making that object what it is for you now.

Read to each other in class.

SEPTEMBER 20

We read Dick's story about his Grandpa's brown leather arm chair this evening, and after talking about it, tried the activity he suggests: writing about something important to you. I wrote about my Grandmother's engagement ring which she gave to me when I graduated from college and which I have worn ever since except for those times when I was either gaining weight or dieting so that there was no finger the ring fitted properly. The ring means a lot to me because I am named after Nana and, growing up in the same house with her as the eldest granddaughter, I learned some of the things I am proudest of from her. Unfortunately, I was very dissatisfied with what I had written. Also, even as I write about this now I am feeling sad. I miss her and haven't figured out how to say that yet.

Willy was fairly happy with what he wrote and he read it to the class.

 This writing I am going to dedicate to my dad. It's kind of odd because I never call him dad. His name is Earl but I call him Eli. Eli is a nickname he picked up when I was about 12 years old—maybe 13. He had and still has one hell of a workshop in his basement and he's always downstairs working on something. One Sunday my friend John Jaconis came over to watch football—it was a playoff game and we couldn't wait for that day because I had been rooting for the Green Bay Packers and he was an old Dallas fan—Green Bay won by the way. Anyway John came over about 11 o'clock and asked where my dad was. I told him that he was down in the basement working on something. He went to the basement steps and yelled out—Hey Eli Whitney, are you going to be down there all day inventing something?—ergo, Eli.
 I'll never forget when I was about 8 years old. The big thing on the block was to see who could build the fastest Go-Kart. We didn't have motors on them but the alley was long and steep so a good push at the top would give you a long ride. Well, we built a wooden Kart but when the boards got splintered from too many ''high speed'' collisions with garage doors and trash cans I decided to employ the aid of my dear father. Needless to say he was thrilled shitless with the thought of spending countless hours making an indestructable Go-Kart. By holding my breath and doing a lot of moaning and groaning I was finally successful in getting his assitance. By now you've probably figured out for yourself that Eli never goes about anything half assed. He decided to build the frame out of 5/8 or 3/4 in tubing, ''For strength.'' The son-of-a-bitch sure was strong. I don't think a run-away Mac Truck could have dented the damn thing. Instead of the old <u>tried and true</u> rope and pulley

18

steering my dad had to work out some elaborate
mechanism of rods and brackets. I must admit
that the steering worked like a champ. The
wheels were ball bearing and the best you could
get. Eli wouldn't even go for a wooden seat.
Hell no, he had to fabricate one out of steel.
When the whole thing was finished it looked like
an antique from WWI. You could just imagine it
with a turret and cannon. Well, when the damn
thing was furnished it took my dad, my mom, my
uncle, my grandmother, my grandfather, and six
of my strongest friends to get it out of the
basement. The big day came and we took it out in
the alley for the big test. I knew we were in
trouble when we stopped on some asphalt (there
was a patch in the alley) and one of the wheels
sunk down in it. It turned out to be the
heaviest, safest, and slowest Go-Kart out on the
alley. I think that I could have run faster
backwards than the Go-Kart would roll. I think
my dad worked on that damn thing for about 2
weeks and he did a great job. It might not have
been too fast but it looked like a new Rolls
Royce sitting next to a derelict from a junk
yard when someone else brought out their kart.

Chapter III

A very difficult notion to get through my head is that words are really just sounds. They don't have any value or meaning—unless we give them meaning or value. I remember how I first discovered this: I was ten and arguing with a friend about when we should run away from home.

"Summer," I said.

"Winter," he said.

"Summer," I retorted.

"Winter," he argued.

"Summer, summer, summer, summer," I screamed. I kept repeating this until I forgot what I meant by the sound: the sound lost all meaning for me.

 Sometime before the next class period, go to someplace that you know will be private for at least two minutes. Repeat the word "summer" for a full two minutes. Time yourself. Don't allow yourself to stop. (If you wish, you might do this together as a class right now.) After your two minutes are up, review the experience. You probably began to say "mer-sum" after a while. Probably the word, even though it remained "summer" for some, lost its meaning; it was just a sound. If it didn't somebody has greater powers of concentration than I.

You see? Those words like "snid" and "rassel" were words as soon as you began using them and agreed what they would stand for. If everybody agrees more or less that the things which we now know as "babies" will be known as "filbs" from now on, "filbs" they will be. Or "chairs" or "bricks" or "plegs" or "travelings" or "ors."

But to take a closer look at a difficulty we have with words, let's take a look at how we learn them. When we were kids, our parents, big brothers and sisters, and friends gave us our words. They pointed to an object and said "tree" and we repeated "tree." We went through this routine several times until we felt that we had all the elements of "tree"—enough so that we didn't have to wait to be told; we said "tree" before anybody else did. Sometimes we had it straight; sometimes we said "tree" and Dad said "bush." Pretty soon though, we had a definition for "tree" and one for "bush."

By definition, I don't mean the kind we find in a dictionary; we didn't have to put the definition into words, we just knew. In fact, we probably couldn't put it into words. For example, try to define with words the ideas of "cat" and of "dog." Then try to put the difference into words. But even though you can't put it into words, you surely can tell a cat from a dog. What we had was an idea with limits around it. A bunch of boxes like my Grandpa used to draw, one for the sound "cat," one for the sound "dog," and one for the sound "tree," and one for the sound "bush."

Whenever we saw something that had the appropriate elements in it, we said "cat" or "bird." At first we got some things confused. We were like the little boy I saw at the zoo last week who refused to say anything but "bird" when he looked at the animal that the rest of us called "seal." I suppose he got "wings" and "flippers" mixed up. But of course his parents were amused, not alarmed, because they knew that soon he'll see the elements that make up the box for the animal that we call "bird" and those that make up the definition for the animal we call "seal."

So by the time we were five, we had a good stock of definition-boxes and their appropriate sounds to help us get ideas out of our heads and into other people's heads. When we made the sound "ice cream," we didn't know for sure we'd get what we wanted, but we were pretty certain that Ma didn't think we were asking for what we called "carrots" or "spinach" or "oatmeal." In other words, we knew that some objects fit into the definition-box for the sound "ice cream" and some fit into the one for the sound "oatmeal." We also were sure that the idea of "wall" didn't fit into the definition of "ceiling." The boxes automatically excluded everything that didn't fit.

Not only did we learn that particular sounds applied to particular objects, but we learned that the same thing went for actions too. "Run" didn't go into the definition of "sleep," anymore than "bite" fit into the definition for "kiss." And it also worked for directions: "up" wasn't "down," "into" wasn't "out of." We could go "into" pajamas and then "into" bed, but we had to stay "out of" Dad's liquor and "out of" Ma's china closet. We also found out very early the difference between the ideas the baby-sitter had when she said "yes" and when she said "no" or when Dad said "good" and when he said "bad."

What a beautiful, simple, and clear world. A definition for everything and everything in its definition.

But of course it wasn't that simple for very long—if indeed it ever really was. Sometimes some of the sounds confused us. When I was sick, the doctor told me the shot and the medicine were "good," but the feeling and the taste certainly didn't fit into the box I had for the sound "good." Or else as a small child you overheard the policeman tell the motorist to get his car "the hell out of here." The driver seemed to get the idea, so it looked like another box was all set. Then that night at supper you asked Dad to get the turnips the hell off your plate. Quite a different effect and the box sprang a leak. Another "breakdown in communication."

What we were learning was not just about words, though, but about objects or ideas—about reality as we were seeing it, and about how the words are related to that reality. We were beginning to discover that some concepts just don't go into nice, neat categories: "love," "fun," "pretty," "good," "grief," to name a few, just don't stay put.

To see why, all we have to do is look back at how we learned the definition in the first place. You had one set of experiences to form the definition for the sound "naughty," and each of your friends had different (though maybe similar) sets. In fact, every time you had an additional experience with the sound "naughty," it came to mean something just a little bit different from what it meant before. In order to get perfect communication, you and your friend will have to list all the times "naughty" was used to describe an action and, of course, by the time you were five you had forgotten most of them. All you have left is a definition without very clear limits.

The solution is to sit with one another and try to get the definition of "naughty" to be about the same size and shape. We try to get others to try to understand what our friends mean by "hate," "just," and "delicious." At first we are less successful with our definitions, but as our linguistic age gets on we do, hopefully, understand others' sounds more and they, hopefully, understand our sounds more. Even if we know that what we mean by "important" is not exactly what the other guy means, we can be fairly confident that we're close enough.

When we can't be so confident, we go off to our private brown leather armchairs and eat candy corn and smell beer, onions, and cigar smoke and think about how we can share our worlds through definitions as communicative as we can make them.

In the meantime it's important to remember that words don't really stand for things, they stand for ideas, for categories, for groups. We learn these groups by learning to label some specific things, but the fact is that my group-category-idea will differ slightly from yours. As a result, one of the basic principles of communication is that the writer must work to provide enough information to the reader so that s/he can understand exactly what the writer wishes.

 ACTIVITY: Choose someone you know who is fun to be around. Write about that person till you are satisfied that any reader will know him/her the way you do. After you finish, read it to someone to satisfy yourself that you have communicated. Now write on a separate piece of paper "_____is fun to be

around." Notice that the one sentence is all you need to write for you to understand, but the whole paper is what someone else would need.

Choose a word like "chair," "cloud," "apple," "giraffe," or "ring." Then write what it means to you so your reader will understand what your particular definition of that word is.

SEPTEMBER 22

Dick called me at 9:15 this morning as I was reading Dear Abby and drinking my tea. One thing I love about teaching evenings is that I can drink tea in the morning without rushing and pretend for a few minutes that I do not work for a living. Dick's call didn't start out to be work but here it is in my journal which is currently part of my work.

Ursula, Dick's youngest daughter, had written to him, enclosing her autobiography which she had written for school, and of which she is quite proud. Dick was delighted by Ursula's piece and so read it to me. So, here I am, putting it in the journal of this class even though Ursula is a little young for Freshman Comp.

Just the other day I was writing about how we select details according to their importance to us as writers and here's Ursula's whole life laid out one detail per year.

         The Autobiography of Ursula Friedrich
                    by Ursula Friedrich

My name is Ursula Anne.

My oldest sister's name is Lisa Marie, my second sister's name is Julie Ann, my brother's name is Lawrence Vincent (Larry). My mother's name is Alice Anne. My father's name is Richard Paul.

When I was 23 I got married. April 10 1990, my husband's name is Donald Brill.

We had 2 girls and 2 boys. My oldest child is Carol Beth, my second to oldest is Donald Junior (D.J.) my third to oldest is Sarah Ann and my youngest is Ricky Tim. All of our kids got married and had there own kids, Donald passed away. In the year he died was 2050 at the age 84.

After he (Donald) died I didn't do very well and had 2 heartattacks and was rushed to the hospital, but, at the arival of the hospital I was already dead. I died at the age of 84, the year 205 1.

All my kids died later on and moved into our old house.

Know I am going to tell you about my younger ages 1-10 Starting out with 1: When I was one 1/2 my mother and father got a divorce. Know with two: When I was two I learned to say Sockie, my sister Lisa's nick name because my brother Larry could not pronounce Lisa's name there for I called her Sockie. Know with three: When I was three I started to walk on my own with out falling. Know with four: When I was four I went out in the winter with: rollar scates and shorts and short sleave shirt and tights and down to the park I went and slipped on ice, my chin cracked. Know for 5: When I was five I had to move to illinois with my Grandma for about 2 months just me noone els because my mom was in the hospital for a back operation. Know for six: When I was six I stepped on a needle while I was barefoot and jumping on our couch. had to have stiches on my left heel. Know for 7: When I was seven my whole family moved to the west side of Madison from the east side. Know 8: When I was eight I had the mumps for two LONG weeks how misserable I was and felt. Know 9: When I was nine I started violin it is a very interesting insterment to play and learn about. Know last but not least 10: When I was ten I road on a air plain for my very first time. Boy was I exited. Well I have nothing more to tell you but I will be writing more books like this.

Chapter IV

We all have separate languages, or at least separate vocabularies. Because I have learned my own words as a result of the experiences I have had in contact with those sounds, and since my experiences must differ from yours, then the definitions I have will necessarily be somewhat different from the definitions you have. What I understand by "boy" might be quite different from what you understand; my definition of "sour" will depend on what foods I've eaten that have been called "sour" how I see a scene as "funny" will depend on what has happened to me or in front of me that has been called "funny."

I remember, for example, a joke that was popular some time ago: "What's the difference between a carload of babies and a carload of bowling balls?" The answer was "You can't use a pitchfork to unload the bowling balls." I remember hearing, and even participating in, arguments about whether or not that joke was "funny"—and therefore to be laughed at. Well, I thought it was not at all "funny," and others thought it was indeed very "funny." Clearly "funny" was being defined differently by each of us and the argument, as the Buddha says, "leads not to enlightenment."

Of course some words "mean" about the same to most of us because the things we have had connected with those sounds are more or less the same. For example, the little boy who called a "seal" a "bird" is sooner or later going to see enough animals which the rest of us call "birds" and enough which we call "seals" so that he'll begin to call the different animals by the names that the rest of us use. But he'll probably always see a connection between the two sets of animals that the rest of us never noticed. (I wonder how many who have read this story will ever see the flippers on the seal the same way again.) So his understanding of the word will vary slightly from others' concept of the same word.

But there are many words which we do not have the same *degree* of agreement about. For instance, when I grew up, some acts were called "tickling." Now I always understood a "tickle" to be the gentle dragging of somebody's fingernails across my back—or really my sister's back, because she's the one who always wanted Daddy to "tickle" her. It was a pleasant experience for her—you could tell by the sounds she made and the look on her face and by the way she usually fell to sleep.

Then, some years later, I found out that to some people "tickle" meant sticking the tickler's finger into the ticklee's ribs—an act that got no happy sounds or pleasant smiles and certainly never put anybody to sleep. So I found out that my definition of the word was different from somebody else's. Who was right with the word? Who was wrong? Nobody, of course. It was just that at that point in my life, my experiences with "tickle" (the sound) differed from somebody's else's. That discovery, naturally, was another experience with the word, and so my definition changed a little. And when you think about it, every time you or I use a word we are using it in (at least) a slightly different way than we ever used it before—and every time we hear a word it is being used in a way we have never heard it before. The point is that not only is my vocabulary different from everybody else's, to some degree; it is different even from mine!

And if "tickle" isn't enough of a problem to think about this way, think about "good." Every time you or I use that word we use it as though we all agree on what "good" means so we can attach it to some object: "It's a 'good' painting," I say. Or "it's a 'good' idea." Or "it's a 'good' essay." But really what I'm talking about is myself. When I say "That was a really fine movie," you might think that I'm talking about the movie, and in a small way, I am. But I'm really talking about me. I'm really saying that the movie is similar to a lot of other experiences (other movies, reviews, classes, conversations, etc., etc.) that I have hooked up to the sound "good." All those past experiences are gone except in my memory and my memory is, of course, a part of me. The movie, too, is part of my memory, so what I'm doing when I say "That was a really fine movie," is tying together two chunks of my mind.

Another problem is that these statements make "good" seem like a quality which everybody understands the same way as they do "green." But, of course, it's really silly to think of "good" as a quality universally agreed on. In fact "green" isn't really the same from one person to another. I have a sport coat (some insist it's a "blazer") which Ursula insists is "brown." She wants me to wear brown slacks with it and tan shirts. To me it's "green." So I wear slacks which we agree are "green," and shirts which likewise we both call "green." But the coat? Well, to one of us it's "green" and to one of us it's "brown."

So usually, if you want to get down accurately what your idea of a "good" something or other is, you'll want to show it fitting into what you think of as "good." Last summer, when my kids were writing one rainy afternoon, Julie wanted to use the typewriter, but Lisa was already there. So, Lisa got to stay there till she was finished. Julie didn't like my decision so much, so she wrote the following:

The story of my Dad
my Dad is a funny ~~A~~
MaN. He is nise
evin if He dusint
let me ~~it~~ tibe.

He makes nise
dinner and. They are
good. and if They are
no good my Dad dusint
make me eat it. I Love my
Dad. an evin if He dusnot
let me have some munny forme zoo.

Love Julie

What she has down is her idea of what a nice Dad is. At that moment she seems to have the definition centered pretty much around eating, doesn't she? She's saying that to her the eating part is more important (as a part of what is nice) than letting her type, or giving her money for the zoo. That's what I mean when I say that the writer might seem to be talking about something else, but all you really have for a subject is yourself.

 Now, in groups, compose papers on what constitutes "good" times, "good" students, "good" children, or "good" food: Be careful: don't worry about what "everybody" or "society" or "teachers" think your subject is. Not unless you think that you can get into their minds and share all of their experiences with the sound "good." Use your own group definition of the word—you'll undoubtedly have to think about it for a "good" long time, but you know that you do have some concept of "good" because you use it all the time. What you'll have to do is think for a bit, then get together with the others in the group and exchange definitions.

SEPTEMBER 25

I was chatting with one of my colleagues, Sally Souder, before class this evening. We were rehashing a faculty meeting that had taken place in the afternoon and the upshot of the conversation was that I got to class almost ten minutes late. When I got into the room, the students ignored me for awhile so I apologized for making them wait and berated myself for not watching the time. I started to fret that the combination of my lateness and preoccupation with the events of the faculty meeting would take their toll on the class and I was covering my distress by taking attendance very officiously when Willie Theis asked if we were going to continue with the same assignment we had been working on last class. I hadn't really planned to, primarily because I had been displeased with my own writing and not because of any particularly sound pedagogical logic. But before I said anything, Willy was opening up his notebook and telling the other

class members that he had gone home after class last
week and re-written the story about his father and
the go-kart.

So what could I do but listen, along with
everyone else, as he read his new version.

ELI'S GO-KART

It was the summer of 1958. I had just
crossed the finish line and won the semi-final
round of our weekly go-kart races. I would now
only need to beat Rich in the final run for the
championship of the block. I was just applying
the brakes, please take the word loosely, and
starting to slow down when a car turned the
corner and left me only 50 feet or so to stop.
Now the alley is not the best place to hold a
go-kart race but it was the best we had. The
brakes that I mentioned before, were of the
tennis shoe variety and were not the best for
quick stops. I had only two choices to make. It
was either the car in front of me or the garage
doors on either side. I chose the garage doors
on the left which proved to be a little harder
than I had anticipated. When the gang finally
reached me, I was laying in the alley on my back
with the front wheel of my kart resting on my
chest. The rest of the kart was still stuck to
the garage door like a piece of gum sticking on
the underside of a table. Needless to say, the
go-kart was a total loss. My friends and I
carried its remains back to my garage and threw
everything in a corner. I told them thanks and
went into the house to brood.

At quarter to 5 Eli got home from work and
saw what was left of my kart in the garage. Eli
is my father. He acquired his nickname from my
friend John. It seemed that whenever John came
to the house Eli would always be in his workshop
in the basement. My dad always has had quite a
workshop and he's very proud of his tools. One
Sunday John came over and not seeing my dad,

31

knew immediately where he was. He went to the basement steps and yelled down ''Hey, Eli Whitney are you still down there inventing?'' Ever since then we've called him Eli.

Anyway, as I was saying, Eli got home from work and when he saw my kart he knew how bad I'd be feeling. He came into my room and we talked for awhile. He knew that I'd spent a long time making my kart and told me not to worry because he'd help me build another one.

Now my go-kart was built from wood that was found in the alleys around the neighborhood. About the fanciest part of the whole thing was the wheels which were ''borrowed'' from a couple of dollys that the local Pepsi-Cola drivers use. The steering was a piece of clothes line and the seat was an old chair with the legs cut off. I mentioned the brakes before or should I say the lack of them.

That night we went down to Eli's workshop and started on my new kart. For a frame Eli decided on steel tubing. It was very strong and he said I'd never bend it. The wheels were ball bearing type and the best Eli could afford. Next came the steering. He didn't think much of my steering, so he made up some complicated arrangements much like a car uses. The seat was formed from aluminum and upholstered with some heavy cloth my mom had sitting around. Next came the ultimate-brakes on both wheels on the back. When everything was assembled, Eli painted it black. It took almost two weeks to finish the kart but when it was finished it was well worth the wait.

Needless to say, I was the envy of the neighborhood and I could have made a fortune by charging my friends a nickel for a ride. It was like having a new Corvette when everyone else was driving an Edsel.

I think that Eli knew I really liked it too, because even though our go-kart craze only lasted for two summers I kept that kart in the

garage until I was 15 years old. It did little
more than collect dust in the corner but
whenever I was out in the garage I'd just have
to take a minute or two just to sit in it.

When he finished, I asked Willy why he had
revised the paper. He said he had been really
pleased with the first version but that when I said
that I didn't like what I had written about my
grandmother he got to thinking that maybe he hadn't
really told the story the way he wanted to.
The whole thing made me feel pretty good. Even
though it's early in the semester, I try to make it
clear that revision is a part of writing and I guess
that Willy understood.

Chapter V

The need for interpretation is inherent in the nature of words and the categories they stand for.

To see this clearly, recall the definition boxes I referred to earlier. Remember how they got their peculiar shapes? You heard a sound in connection with a variety of objects—let's say "green"—and soon you yourself were seeing things which you named "green" without any help.

You had to pull out of all the objects whatever it was they had in common—whatever you could guess constituted "green." Something about the grass, your shirt, your uncle's car, your mother's shoes, that ball you liked to play with, the wallpaper at the foot of your bed. Something about each of them made everybody say "green" in connection with them. You came onto an idea of what it was—the sensation you experienced when light came to you within a certain range on the spectrum. (Of course, you didn't know any of that; all you knew was the experience.)

But then, finally, you had learned what "green" is. Right? And now you know what "green" is Right?

Maybe not.

Let's just stop for a moment and think. Just exactly what is "green"? "Green" is a series of lines which stands for a series of sounds which stands for a concept which exists in my mind as a result of the experiences which I have had in connection with that series of sounds.

You might want to stop and think about that and discuss it.

Here's what I think happened to give you your ideas of "green." As you grew up and as objects were referred to as "green," the exact points where "green" met "blue" and where "green" met "yellow" moved back and forth. And they still do. Taking the color spectrum, the colors "green," "blue," and "yellow" lie something like this (I'm using "black" on "white" printing instead of the color spectrum on purpose. If we used a color spectrum we could easily get off the point by talking about whether I was "right" or "wrong" about what color is what.)

In other words my definition has kind of hazy lines.

Now, since your definition is based on your experiences, your equally fuzzy definitions will probably be a bit to the left and/or right of mine, because your experiences with "green" must be different from, though perhaps similar to, mine.

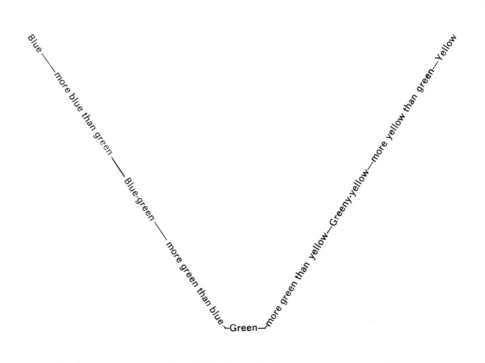

So, that's part one of the difficulty with the categories created by words—something which we've considered a good deal before. Still, no matter how much we discuss it and maybe even believe it, when we write we're sure our words must mean the same to everybody—but, in fact, everybody's definitions are a bit different from everybody else's.

That's enough of a problem, but there's a part two of the category difficulty. Part two has to do not so much with the differences between people's definitions, but with the fuzziness of the definitions themselves. We act very much as though "green" refers to a definable space on the color spectrum, that it's the job of a language user to accept the world as his language presents it to him. We think that there is a color "green" because there is a word green. But the truth, as we have seen, is that the difference between green and yellow (that is, the point on the spectrum at which we're no longer talking about "green," but about "yellow") is not a clear point, but a very hazy and shifting range. What makes it "green" is not some characteristic which is measurable and concrete. No, what makes it "green" is being called "green."

We think there is a definite point until we look closer. It's like smoke when we get close up: where does the "smoke" end and the "air" begin?

The point is that our language makes us think, and thus act, like the universe was made up of a bunch of definable, categorizable things, ideas, and relationships. But, while I sometimes think I can tell where my typewriter comes in contact with the kitchen table it's sitting on right now and I don't get the two mixed up ever, part of the universe is made up of reality which is not so categorizable.

Here's another activity to make this more clear. Put your index finger on your wrist.

Next, touch your forearm.

Now put your finger on your elbow.

You have now put your finger on your wrist, then on your forearm, finally on your elbow.

Take a pencil and draw a line exactly where your wrist becomes your forearm and where your forearm becomes your elbow. Do the same for your chin, jaw, neck, and shoulder. Do you have a chin? A jaw? Can you put your finger on your face and not be sure whether you're on chin or jaw? (I was going to say, "Is there an area on your face which you're not sure is chin or jaw?" But that would have made it seem possible to locate the "area" exactly—and of course, that can't be done either.)

Our language makes it seem that there is a definable point or line between one category and another—between blue, green, and yellow; between wrist and arm and arm and elbow; between walk and run; between run and dash; between tall and short; between fat and skinny; between white and black; between right and wrong; between good and bad; true and false; pleasure and pain; dumb and smart; between a lot of pairs.

Discuss: What is the difference between _____ and _____? (Fill in with any of those pairs above—or pairs of your own choosing.)

Chapter VI

It seems to me that there is a natural and unavoidable conflict between people. Since language (especially vocabulary) is so unstatic, so unlike what we'd guess from dictionaries, we have a built-in difficulty when we try to communicate.

The dictionary makes it seem that words are fixed, set, decided, neat. Don't blame the dictionaries; they've got enough trouble; what I'm saying is that they have a built-in difficulty: the book is printed at a point in time so they have to do the best they can. Nonetheless, words don't mean the way dictionaries make them seem to. They're like waves on the ocean: moving (or are they really?), trading water with the neighbor waves (or do they really?), and finally breaking up and disappearing (or did they ever really exist as separate things?—what is a "wave," by the way?).

We think of waves as separate things, don't we? They look like this: ⌣⌣⌣ What does one wave look like? ⌣ or ⌢ ? Or is part of what I've just drawn a hunk from surrounding waves? Think about them as they exist on the ocean instead of in my drawings. Here, there, gone, back, up, down, swell, shrink, move, explode, wiggle—they do all these things pretty much at the same time.

Just as we're used to thinking about the waves as separate and distinct identities when they really aren't we think about words as separate, definable, and defined when they really aren't.

The dictionary definition of a word is like a picture of a wave. It's not really the wave and it doesn't really communicate the "reality" of the wave. But it does give somebody who hasn't seen one before an idea of what one is; the picture and the definition give someplace to start from in understanding the wave and the word. It's just that we shouldn't get the picture and the wave mixed up.

Strange, but true: words are just like we are: constantly changing, moving, shifting. I hear from my science friends that, while I slept last night, my body added whole bushels of new cells—so I'm not the same as I was last night when I went to sleep. The guy who is writing these words won't exist by the time you are reading them. All I've got to hold me together is my memory of what I was and what I thought at one time—and that memory is constantly changing.

Discuss: Think about your changes—how do you change physically from moment to moment?

Discuss: Think about your changes—how do you change physically from moment to moment?

How do you change mentally? Emotionally? Are these changes separate from each other? Are they all part of the same change?

Here's a piece Julie wrote about how nice her brother is.

MY BROTHER

MY BROTHER   IS   A NISE BROTHER BE   CAUSE HE DUSINT   RELY   GET MAD   AT   ME AND   HE PLAYS , WITH ME   IN THE   POOL   AND   HE HELPS   ME   ON SADR   DAY WHEN   I WANT TO MIX   MY SILLY   SAND THAT   MY   DADY SENDED   ME .   AND   HE IS NOT MEN TO   ME LIKE   SOME   OF HIS   FRIENDS   ARE WHEN THEY TESE ME.   AND HE LETS ME   EAT SOME OF HIS COTEN CANDY   WHEN   I DROPED MINE.

by Julie   friedric
                                    h

Is this the same "nice" as before? (See p. 29) Has Julie changed? Is her idea of "nice" different from what it was? Are there two different aspects of "nice" for Julie? For you? Is there one "nice" and different applications of it? Or is "nice" not just one word—that is, does "nice" change from situation to situation?

Discuss: Are you "you" now? or then? when? Or are you going to be "you"? What does "you" mean? What does "you" mean to you?

What do you mean to you?

Write: Tell about an experience during which you felt like "you." Write about one during which you didn't feel that way.

When you write about that experience, deal with the elements that made it seem to be you, and those elements that made it seem not to be you.

Write about something you used to like, but don't any more. See if you can remember why you liked it. Get into groups and read your paper to the others. Discuss how you are different now from before. Be sure to discuss if you're better off now. (I, for example,

used to enjoy watching baseball, but I no longer do. Am I better or worse off? What do "better" and "worse" mean? Or, for another example, I never used to enjoy "classical" music. Now I do. Again—am I better or worse for the change?)

Discuss: If you can't stand still, how can you expect a word to stand still? If you're changing so fast, and if your words and your friends and your friends' words are wiggling around like this, why do you bother to use words? Why not just communicate without words?

SEPTEMBER 27

In class tonight, I played George Carlin's comedy monologue ''The Seven Words You Can't Say on Television.'' As I hoped this led to a rather lengthy discussion of what makes words ''dirty'' and the opposite, what makes words ''clean.'' Several students got into an argument about whether it was all right to call a woman a ''broad.'' Interestingly, those who thought it was a perfectly neutral word were men and those who contended that it was highly charged and derogatory were women.

I was a bit worried as the class wrangled on that I had introduced the concept too early in the semester. That the students weren't ready yet to recognize that there is nothing inherently good or bad about a word. That a word is not identical with the thing it represents. Then, wouldn't you know, someone said ''Sticks and stones may break my bones but words will never hurt me.''

We started talking about whether or not words really can hurt a person. So I asked the students to take a few minutes and think about whether or not they had ever been hurt by a word. I suggested that they jot down what they came up with.

When the class members started to read from their paragraphs I was relieved to discover that about half of them were making the distinction between being hurt by the intention of the speaker which informed those words. In fact, the students who were irate that I would play a record in which someone said aloud the seven deadly words were writing about words that were not even on the list. Tanya Shifrin, who emigrated with her husband and young son from Russia less than a year ago, read this to us:

My mother called me callous, when I decided to leave my country and parents. It made me powerless to object to her. This is her opinion. I think this is error. Because I must be with my family (my husband and son). If my husband decided to leave Russia and he decided that it will be better for future of our son, I agree with him. Because I love him and I know, he always thinks about subject very much and after that he does the decision.

I left class feeling that at least some of the students understood that it isn't so much that a word is dirty but that the purpose and intention behind the word is the hurtful thing.

SEPTEMBER 28

Rosie Pressley brought her journal in yesterday. She missed class last week because one of her children was sick and she couldn't leave him alone. As I was reading what she had written, I was struck by how what she had written was an example of what Dick means when he says that our definitions are made up of our experiences. Rosie had written a piece called ''Loneliness'' in which she explains loneliness through some very specific experiences she has.

Loneliness

Loneliness is being without you
Loneliness is missing your touch
Loneliness is spending the nights alone
Loneliness is listening to the children
run around the house with noise but
the house is still empty

Loneliness is hating to go to bed
Because when I do I always dream of you
Loneliness is when you get up in the
morning and no one to say good morning
to but the pillow

Loneliness is cooking oatmeal for the
children for breakfast, instead of your
favorite of bacon, eggs, toast, and coffee
or maybe grapefruit, bacon and coffee

Loneliness is remembering the wonderful
times we had together
Loneliness is going to the phone wanting
to phone you but something inside says
No

Loneliness is when one of the
children ask ''Mama where is Daddy?''

Loneliness is trying to figure out
what went wrong with our love.

Chapter VII

Here are a couple of activities which are designed to show you right away if you've been successful in communicating or not.

 Put your name on a piece of paper. Then go outside and hide it somewhere. You might want to take notes on the way out and the way back, because when you come back you'll write directions to get somebody to where your name is and back to the classroom. After everybody is finished writing, put all the papers in a pile and let each person take one. Follow the directions. After everybody is back, either with a name or without, let each direction-follower tell the author of his/her directions what happened when s/he followed the directions. The rule here: The author cannot talk, only listen. Here's why. The tendency will be to say to someone who had trouble at the steps, "Oh, well what I meant for you to do was. . . ." That, of course, misses the whole point of the activity. What you want to know as author is *only* "Where did my reader have trouble with my directions?" And the next step is to go ahead and change the directions so that somebody else doesn't have the trouble. Remember, don't try to blame anybody—either the follower for being stupid, or yourself for writing bad directions. Just find any confusion and fix it up.

One person leave the class for a half hour. Then have the teacher draw a design on the board something like this:

or like this:

or whatever. Then the class organizes into a committee with a chair-person and a writer. The goal is for the whole class to produce one set of directions written for the person who left the room. When that person returns, the only one allowed to make a sound is the writer of the committee and the only sounds s/he can utter are ones that are written on paper. No one else in class can speak, giggle, grunt or give any help to the directions follower. The idea is to try to make it as realistic as possible. You see, when you write something, usually you don't accompany your writing to be

sure the reader understands. All there is for the reader is your writing. Same thing here, except you have a reader reading out loud and you can watch the effect of your writing.

Write directions on how to play a parlor game. Then, play it in class. Don't explain your directions. Let the class be guided only by what you've written.

OCTOBER 2

In class tonight, the students hid pieces of paper with their names on them and then wrote directions on how to find them. Then students just started approaching each other and just handing out their directions and asking them to follow them. As soon as Willy had hidden his paper and written his directions, he asked me if I would try them out, and I did, and couldn't find the paper and came back to tell him. He then fixed up the directions a little and gave them to someone else who was able to find the paper.

Several people tried to make this easy—they put the papers right outside the door to the classroom, or in some other place that was pretty easy to find, so I asked them to try doing it so that it was more challenging.

Carol asked me to try her directions, and I did. They were explicit, and written in an easy-to-follow, step-by-step way, so I got down to the basement without much trouble, and then over to the pay phone, and zeroed in on her paper. I took the paper from behind the phone and brought it back to her. I didn't say that she did a good job, or that her directions were ''clearly written'' or make any comment at all. I simply handed her the paper, and smiled. That was all it took. She smiled, and I could see she was very pleased that she had been able to explain this to me.

I have one student who asks me all the time how ·
he's doing, and if his papers are ''well written.''
I never know what, if anything, is communicated by
the expression ''well written'' on a student's
papers, but this student obviously believes it means
something other than merely ''I like it,'' and kept
after me to find out if his papers were ''well
written.'' One of his papers was a paper of
directions, so I asked him if the person he had
given his directions to had been able to get where
he wanted him to go. He said ''yes,'' but apparently
it still didn't dawn on him that that answered the
question about whether the paper was ''well
written.'' Finally, he asked me what grade I thought
he was to get, and I said I didn't know, and I asked
him what grade he thought he deserved. After I said
that, I was sorry I had said it, because I don't
think this particular student is ready to handle the
idea that he might have something to say about his
own grade.

But Carol understood right away what I was
saying to her when I returned the slip of paper with
her name on it and smiled at her. That was all it
took. I could see her thinking, ''I did it. It
worked.''

OCTOBER 3

Butch Wade turned in his journal last night. He
had written about the direction writing activity and
I was pleased to see that he was starting to develop
some understanding of the author's responsibility in
communication. But more than that, it's clear from
this entry that Butch is really thinking about how a
person writes, dealing with at least one important
question: how much can you simplify and clarify
without losing what you are trying to say.

Wade's Journal

In class the other day we had to draw, or rather Angela drew a picture and we had to write some directions so that a classmate named Pat could understand and draw the picture exactly like Angela had drawn before. Well, I had to be in a group with three chicks and you know how that situation usually turns out. Well the two other girls let the one lady who was very outspoken but very seldom makes sense. Well instead of taking charge like I knew I should have I thought it would be better since I was not getting a grade to let the outspoken one have her way. Well, as usual, she didn't write the directions too clearly and the result of the test was disastrous. So we had some home work in which we were to write some directions on to another design. I tried it with my little brother and his girlfriend. The first time they didn't make the design I wanted them to so I guess it was my fault. The second time my little brother got the design although his girlfriend didn't so that means that my directions wasn't as clear as it could possibly be.

Now that brings up another point. Maybe my direction was as simple as they could be. I mean there is probably a point where the directions can get no more simpler. Hey if you say that you have four fingers and one thumb how can you make that point any clearer. So maybe my directions were as clear as they could be because I usually try to write as simple as I can.

Chapter VIII

One of my assignments in class some time ago was for the students to show me without words something about themselves. Some dressed up, others played music, and one student, Ettie Ciment, brought the following drawing.

 ACTIVITY: What do you think she's saying about herself? (1) Put yourself in her place and write what you feel like. (2) Bring a picture to the next class (photograph or drawing) which expresses something about you. (If you don't want to use a picture, do something else—bring a record, do a dance, read a poem.) Write an explanation of the picture—explain how the picture relates to you.

OCTOBER 9

Tonight we began the assignment where everyone brings in a poem, a record, a picture, or whatever seems to communicate something about themselves. One woman brought in a leaf from a Wandering Jew plant and explained that since she was back in school she felt just like this plant, turning to whatever light was offered, thriving and sending out new shoots all the time. She said that she felt she had begun a whole new life.

Don Hensley presented us with the following piece—I don't know whether to call it a cartoon, a

poem, a picture, or what, but maybe I just shouldn't
try to label it. We all enjoyed it after puzzling a
bit, but I still haven't figure out quite what to
call it.

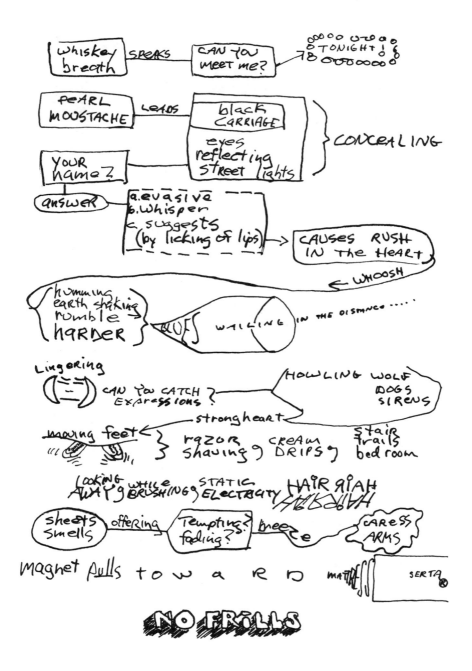

whiskey breath — SPEAKS → CAN YOU MEET ME? → TONIGHT!

PEARL MOUSTACHE — LEADS → black CARRIAGE / eyes reflecting street lights } CONCEALING

YOUR NAME? — answer → a. evasive / b. whisper / c. suggests (by licking of lips) → CAUSES RUSH IN THE HEART ← WHOOSH

humming earth shaking rumble HARDER → WAILING IN THE DISTANCE.....

Lingering — CAN YOU CATCH EXPRESSIONS? — strongheart — HOWLING WOLF DOGS SIRENS

moving feet ← } RAZOR shaving ☞ CREAM DRIPS ☞ stair trails bedroom

looking AWAY ☞ while BRUSHING ☞ STATIC ELECTRICITY HAIR RIAH

sheets smells — offering — Tempting? fading? — breeze — CARESS ARMS

magnet pulls toward mattress SERTA®

NO FRILLS

51

her whiskey possessed breath told me
to meet her later on tonight.
best a panhandled moustache led
to a glossy black carriage concealing
the brown eyes reflecting street
lights. I ask her name —
she whispers & licks her
lips leaving a wet rosey sheen
as my heart dropped & my hand felt
hollow — the music was thrumming
harder — m blues harmonica wailing
in the distance..... expression too
escapes me as I linger about looking
such a fright howling dogs
don't say no... strength falls
feet & they begin to move the
shaving cream drips off my chin leaving
a trail up the stairs & into the bedroom
she turns away while brushing
static hair. white sheets and musk
smells offer temptation fades away
softly into the breeze as she tenderly
caresses my arms pulled me toward
a heavy dark mattress "no frills"
read a sign posted on the backboard

her whiskey possessed breath told me to meet her
later on tonight, but a pearl handled moustache
led to a glossy black carriage, concealing the
brown eyes reflecting street lights. I asked her
name—she whispered & licked her lips leaving a
wet rosey sheen—my heart dipped, my head felt
hollow—the music was drumming harder—blues
harmonica wailing in the distance . . .
expression escapes me as I linger about. howling
dogs just don't say no . . . strength shoots
thru my feet as they begin to move. shaving
cream drips off my chin leaving a trail up the
stairs & into the bedroom. she turns away while
brushing static hair. white sheets and muck
smells offer temptation that fades away softly
into the breeze as she tenderly caresses my arms
pulls me toward a smooth heavy mattress ''no
frills'' read a sign posted on the back board.

I'm always a bit nervous about this assignment
because it can be very intense and personal (and
sometimes unusual) but I keep doing it because it
seems always to produce a good writing.
    Several people asked Clare Christopher to read
her paper; and when they saw my puzzled expression,
Pat volunteered that Clare had been re-writing her
piece before class so she and Gary and Ralph had
already heard it and liked it.
    ''I couldn't really bring in my object,'' Clare
said. ''You'll see why. And I suppose the object
really explains something about when I was little
but I guess it tells something about me now. And
it's more of a poem than anything else. So here
goes.'' Clare had said this all in one breath.

''Worms''

Worms, I woke up.
I felt them crawling inside of me.
I lay there hypersensitive
to every movement
that my body made.
I was ten then.
Silent tears streamed down my face.
It was late
but how could I sleep when
the worms were gnawing
at my ribs
chewing my stomach.
My tears fell to the pillow
I couldn't sleep.

Worms. I woke up Mom
bleary eyed she sighed
And listened as
I told her again
about the worms.
She made tea and talked to me.
I tried to listen
but I knew.
Mrs. Wetzle at school
had told us about those worms.
And I knew
Because lots of times
I didn't wash my hands
And I played
in barefeet

Worms. I could feel them there
I couldn't sleep.
Crawling in me
Gnawing at my ribs.
I couldn't sleep.
they had entered my feet.
I could feel them there.
I had them for years.

Fran Ostrander raised her hand after we had finished
groaning about Clare's worms. I knew something was
up because Fran usually just talks when she has
something to say. So I asked her what she had
brought in for the class. She said ''I didn't bring
in anything, I just wrote something, I hope it's
okay.''

''Read it, and we'll find out.'' I answered.

''I call it 'Death's Lesson.' It's about my
father.''

And Fran started to read.

Death's Lesson

My father was a very big influence in my
life. He taught me how to live my life to its
fullest, and taught me the importance of being
the best person you can be no matter what that
happens to be. In addition to that, on May 2nd,
1977, at the age of 61, my father showed me how
to die.

He was sick for a few years prior to his
death. From 1974-1976 he was in and out of
several hospitals being seen by many doctors. No
one could pinpoint just what was wrong. He lived
with weakness, dizziness and abdominal pain and
had to retire at age 60. Then he developed
jaundice and lost 50 lbs. He couldn't eat very
many things. Especially meat. He was nauseated
and vomited quite frequently.

What was bad was that my folks lived in Ohio
and I moved to Mo. when I married my husband. I
wanted to be with my Dad and help him as he
helped me so often in my life. With 600 miles
between us, the best I could do was letter
writing, telephoning and an occasional trip to
Ohio.

On one such trip, in Feb. 77, he had surgery
to determine the cause of his illness. We found
out that he had cancer of the pancreas with
little time left to live. Ironically, I had just
recently found out that I was pregnant with my

first child. God had given me something to cling to in those months of waiting for my father's life to end.

I returned to Missouri at the end of Feb. but my thoughts ever always in Ohio and what was happening there. Phone calls became more frequent between us. The last one came at the end of April just two months after I left Ohio. The call was from my sister, Mary. Dad was hemorrhaging!

I talked to my Dad minutes before he was to leave for the hospital for the last time. He told me, ''it's not good.'' Here was a dying man telling me this so strong and trying to help me. I choked back my tears and told myself that it was my turn to help him. Why should he put up a show of strength for me now? I hung up the phone, packed and got on the next plane. I cried the whole plane ride and prayed to God to let him hold on till I saw him again.

My sister picked me up at the airport when I arrived. She told me to prepare myself for a lot of changes that had taken place in my Dad. I prepared myself well so I could walk in the room and focus on my love for him and what he said and not on what this disease was doing to him.

I am glad I did this because the changes were drastic. He was yellower, skinnier, and weaker but he still had the same smile and out-stretched arms. My mom was there too. My whole life was just like that moment. Close and loving. God chose that moment for me to feel my baby kick for the first time.

The next week would prove to be very confusing for me. I was constantly confronted with life inside me but death staring me in the face. All my emotions were being exercised vigorously. I was feeling a baby kicking and hiccuping but seeing tubes thru my Dad's nose and bile draining from his body, IV fluids running in his arm and life leaving his body. But his mind was working as always.

My father's life was occupied with his 3 favorite things: his wife and children and 15 grandchildren. He was worried about us getting enough sleep. He made my one sister go home because ''his grandchildren needed their mother'' and she spent ''entirely too much time at the hospital even if he did appreciate it.'' He told me he hoped he'd been a good enough father. I had no doubt about that and told him so. He used to tell me to be good at anything I undertake. That covers everything, whether it is being a good wife, mother or student. I was anxious to show him that he had raised a good daughter.

I spent hours at his bedside rubbing his head or giving the backrubs he loved. We talked and reassured each other of the love we shared for each other. I told him of my plans to name my baby after him. We had one week to share together.

Around 11:30 pm May 2nd, my sister Barb and I were at his bedside watching him. He had been knocked out of it for the previous 24 hours with drugs given for pain. I gazed down and saw his chest rise and fall a little slower than before. I ran out and called to my mom, brother and 2 other sisters to come in. My Dad's wish was to leave his life as he lived it; with his family. We stood there for about 2 minutes. It seemed like an eternity.

I remember praying to God to take this man and stop his suffering. His chest stopped moving then and I wanted to scream Breathe—Breathe. But I didn't. He was at rest at last and his ordeal was over. I knew I would be purely selfish and I wasn't raised that way. He had no need for continuing pain but I still had a need for him. A need for his voice, his wisdom and even his teasing or joking around. I cried for him, my mom, me and the baby he would never see.

I was shown how to die with dignity. How to die in the same manner in which you lived so

that the death is just a continuation of one's
life. How to die and still be of help to your
family. That is important because the loved ones
must carry on with living after you're gone.

Four months later, I delivered my son,
Timothy James, who was named after my father. My
goal with him will be to teach him how to live
his life to the fullest and the importance of
being the best person he can be no matter what
that happens to be.

When Fran finished reading, she sat still for a
few minutes. No one said anything for a while, and
then Carol turned to her and said ''Thank You.''

OCTOBER 12

Two nice things happened at school last night.
(You've probably noticed by now that I started this
journal by writing after class each night and I have
drifted into writing about the class the next day. I
suppose it's that by the time I get home, have a
snack and read the newspaper all I want to do is
crawl in bed and watch whatever detective movie is
on television or read whatever detective novel I'm
in the midst of. It's also true that I find it very
difficult to sit still long enough to jot down my
thoughts from the class I'm keyed up from just
having taught.)

So back to the two nice things. First, Pat Young
read a piece she had written in her journal about
learning to sew. And second, as I was cleaning my
desk—something I do once every semester—I found a
line for a poem. I must explain that while many
people who write keep a journal of words, phrases,
subjects, partially written pieces, or whatever, I
keep scraps of paper. The line isn't much by itself
''Every woman should have a lover who leaves no
traces'', but I've been thinking about it since
yesterday and am about ready to see where it might
go as a poem.

Pat's piece about sewing caught my attention because, as well as being a well told story, it reminded me of my own sewing lessons—also from my grandmother and also on a treadle machine. And writing that works is writing that lets us see ourselves in the words of the writer.

I'll stop sewing now and start to work on my journal. Sewing is one of my redeeming hobbies. It is one thing that I pride myself on doing very well. I like to do a lot of things—playing tennis, working on my house, writing (ha), but so few of these things I do well.

I feel very good after I make a dress or a suit. I started sewing when I was a little girl. My grandmother was a dress maker and had learned her trade from her uncle who was a tailor. That was one of the professions that was suitable for a young lady back in the golden days of the early century. It was either that or factory work or else get married and raise a family. Well, since my grandmother and grandfather couldn't afford to get married yet and my grandmother couldn't stand factories, she took up dress making seriously. It wasn't too long before she had built up a sizeable clientelle. Back in those days, ready to wear clothes just weren't readily available. She continued sewing for people even after her and my grandfather were married and even into the depression. That's when my mother was born. Well, despite the depression, my mother was one of the best dressed kids in school. Grandma would sew for the butcher's kids in exchange for meat and that sort of thing. Any materials that were left over would make clothes for my mother and for Grandma and Grandpa. You know how people were back then— they didn't waste a stitch. Well, Grandma kept on sewing and tailoring for people until I was old enough to learn. My mother never cared for sewing and in fact, didn't like to wear home made clothes. It didn't make any difference that the things Grandma made were better than store bought clothes, Mom just didn't like the connotations.

Well, I learned to sew doll clothes just about when I was seven or eight and continued to sew small items—doll clothes and gifty type things even for other people. I didn't really take it up for myself until I was in my second year of high school. I wanted a sewing machine very badly, but we couldn't afford a new one. My father was convinced that it was a passing fancy and that I would loose interest in sewing and then the money paid out for a new sewing machine would be lost. My sister had a second hand treadle sewing machine that was made in 1901 and she gave it to me when her husband bought her an electric model. Well, my dream came true. Every cent of my clothing allowance went to buying material and then I was soon making clothes for my sister, my mother and even doing tailoring for my father. This was all what my Grandmother had taught me. I taught myself further on tailoring by getting books out of the Library and then took Home-Ec in high school for more pointers. Then for my senior year Christmas, my father surprized me with a brand new electric sewing machine, complete with cabinet and a whole bunch of accessories. I was in heaven. Well, I've long since worn out that machine and have a bigger and better model, but I still remember Grandma and my father everytime I sew a skirt or whatever.

I still sew for my mother and do tailoring for people for pay. I have even made winter coats and a suit for my husband. I would like to have more time to sew than what I do now, but I guess if I did it all the time, I wouldn't enjoy it as much as I do now.

Chapter IX

In 1855, a former newspaper editor published a book of poetry. The title page looked like this:

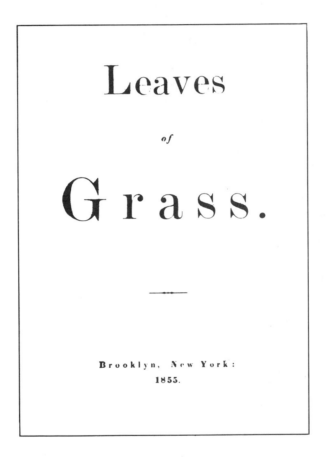

You probably noticed that the author's name is missing; instead of his name, Whitman chose to use the following:

Five years later, when he published a revised edition of the book, this is the way the title page and its facing page looked:

Discuss the difference between the 1855 pages and the 1860 ones. Notice that what you're talking about is self-expression— Whitman saying to the world, "This is me."

There are a good many more ways to express ourselves to the world than by title pages and engravings. One obvious way is by dressing the way we dress. Clothes, like words, can be used as masks. Many times we adopt a style of clothing to hide what we are from people. Elevator shoes, padded shoulders, cosmetics generally, are devices to make ourselves more acceptable to others than we feel we are without the devices. We dress according to what we wish we were and according to what we want others to see in us.

 (1) For the next class decide what you would like others to think of you; then dress so that your classmates will get the point.
(2) Divide into pairs and write about the image you believe your partner is trying to project.

You have been using your clothes to manipulate what others think of you. Another thing you can do with your clothes is to dress any way you want to, that is, to express what you are, as opposed to what you want others (or even yourself) to think of you. Think of what you would wear in that case.

 Write a page or two so that your classmates will see the differences in the two outfits, so they will know the difference between what you wear to impress and what you wear to express.

Do you know people who always seem to dress just for themselves? If you do, you'll probably realize that they seem to be comfortable with themselves. When we feel good about ourselves, then we can dress how we feel; when we fear what others will think, then we dress to avoid others criticisms, then we dress to make them approve of us.

The same thing goes for our style of language. We try to sound fancy whenever we're worried about what the other person thinks of us. In order to relax and sound like ourselves, we have to believe in our own merit and not be worried about what the neighbors will think.

For several weeks, one of the women in the class, Loretta Johnson has been dropping by my office to talk about a paper she is writing. It got started with Dick's brown leather armchair essay when all the members of the class selected some object that was very important to them and tried to tell the rest of the class why it was important. Loretta was not pleased with the way she had written about her treasured possession and kept coming by to talk to me about ways to change or clarify what she had said. Finally, on Monday, she told me that she was satisfied that she had put on paper what she felt the object meant to her.

As I read her final draft, I became more and more conscious that she had succeeded in particularizing the feelings she was writing about and had given her reading audience a careful and vivid sampling of the pictures she carried in her mind when she looked at her Peasant Girl. She had in fact filled in all the blanks so that her readers were not left guessing. She had explored the images and emotions and caught them in pictures that were understandable to others. She had written a really moving piece. I am including it here because I do think that it illustrates what Dick is talking about when he asks us to pay attention to details and present those details to our audience.

Everyone probably thinks their mother's special and I'm no different. I think my mother's special too. Although she died over six years ago, the memory of her is still very real to me. If mothers are supposed to guide and direct our lives in a worthwhile direction and set an example of honesty and decency, then mine has to be rated near the top. Even in her shortcomings, I learned a lot about life and I have tried hard to avoid making some of the mistakes she happened into.

My Mom was truly a fine person, honest, loyal, unselfish and full of human concern. Most of all she was always a lady. She never disgraced her husband or children which in its self is remarkable because my Mom was also an alcoholic. She wasn't always an alcoholic but she was always a great lady and we had every reason to respect her.

Mom would have been more content to be a farmers wife, or if she'd have been born in another generation, she could have been a terrific pioneer lady because she could be very determined and gutsy, loved nature, the soil and all of Gods creatures. I can imagine her living in a log cabin in the woods and thriving on every minute of it. Working hard all day and getting satisfaction from life in keeping her family fed and healthy. Knowing Mom, she probably would have been right out in the fields working with her husband.

But it was Moms fate in life to marry a man who was to become involved in the world of big business. It didn't start out that way but that's how it ended.

Mom always stayed a country girl at heart, even tho she moved to the city with her family when she was 13 years old. Her father had deserted them and she worked in a factory to help out as so many children did during those days of the Depression of the 30's.

And that's where my Dad, who was a tall handsome bachelor met my Mom and was swept off his feet. She was a strikingly beautiful girl of 17 and from the pictures I've seen of her, it's plain to see why he noticed her. It was more than physical beauty but something in the warm dimpled smile and sparkeling eyes that went straight to your heart. Since she was a naive but spunky girl, whose affections only went along with marriage, that's what he did!

A lot happened over their 40 years together. Most of the adjusting had to be on her part. As times got better in the country after World War II, Dad became more and more successful in his job. Mom was so proud of his accomplishments but was saddened too because it meant more traveling and long hours away from home. After the years of struggeling together to get through the hard times of the depression era, it must have been quite a change for Mom to be left alone so much with a young daughter and 2 small sons. In her case, money definetly didn't buy happiness. It was along about this time, that her habit for lonely evening drinking began.

Mom just wasn't a woman of the world and could not have been, nor did she want to be what's called a ''liberated woman.'' So if my Dad's business success meant lonely hours for her, then that's the way it had to be as far as she was concerned. Dad could depend on her to take care of his home and children. It gave her great pride that he could always come home and find her there, with a good home cooked meal waiting for him.

Her home and family were the most important things in the world to her and she was happiest when she was doing nice things for them. She was a terrific cook and used to beam with pride when we enjoyed her good meals.

After I was married and away from home, she still liked us to come to their house for our birthday dinners. They lived about a 2 hour drive from us but we seldom missed going. My birthday is in October and every year when the leaves started to turn, my mouth would start watering for banana cream pie. Mom knew it was my favorite and she'd always fix it for me. Her banana pie was full of sliced bananas, not one or two slices that you can hardly find, like in restaurant pie. The filling was homemade, of course, made with real butter, the crust flaky and tender and the meringue was thick and perfect with toasted coconut on top.

Mom was a folksy, down home type person. She was always her real self, nothing pretend about her and that's why most people loved her and those that didn't weren't worth knowing. She could see right into a person and tell a phony or hypocrite right away and she was outspoken enough to let them know it.

Because of her deep sense of honesty and terrific insight, Mom could really spot an unscrupulous business deal. This could be a great benefit to my Dad at times, except when he had some deals of his own going on that he would have preferred Mom weren't so critical of. He learned to be more cautious on how informed he kept her but the humor of it was he could hardly ever fool her nor could anyone else. She always said she'd rather be poor than have Dad do anything dishonest and I'm sure she meant it. She was happiest during the lean years of the depression when they really needed each other.

No matter how successful Dad got, Moms tastes stayed the same. They lived comfortably but not extravagantly. She enjoyed gifts from the family no matter how small and kept everything we gave her. She even framed a picture our daughter had drawn for her with crayons.

I still find myself wanting to buy some little things I see that I know she'd like. We had lots of little family jokes between us and when I'd see some trinket or card that reminded me of the incident, I'd send it to her. It was sure to make her laugh. She had a deep, hearty, laugh that made you feel warm all over and it made you want to laugh too. Mom never got tired of hearing stories about our children, the only grandchildren she would know. You could tell she really liked to hear all about everything that concerned us, the kinds of things that other people only half listen to and nod politely at.

At long last, Dad sort of semi-retired from his busy job, traveling less and seldom gone for more than a day or so at a time. Mom was a truly contented person again, having Dad at home with her more and since all the kids were gone, they even took some short trips together. Most of all she enjoyed having more time to care for her flower gardens. Their yard had flowers blooming from early spring to late fall. Roses were her specialty. They had long, thick stems and such huge blooms that they looked like florists roses. She really had a way with flowers and I never learned the secret.

The late night drinking had almost stopped by this time, partly because she was content but mostly because the years of alcohol and high blood pressure had taken their toll. Mom never did admit she had a drinking problem, but she had to know she did. Her drinking was done in the privacy of her own home, after every one was settled for the night. She insisted on keeping her addiction to alcohol a private matter and only very close relatives and friends knew of her problem. But she never did allow it to interfere with her responsibilities of a wife and mother. This is remarkable to me and a testimony to the super soul and moral character she was made of. She knew we loved and respected her and never allowed herself to humiliate us or to lose her own self respect. Most people I know who have a serious drinking problem use their condition as an excuse for unbecoming behavior. So she drank in private. The worse thing that happened was that she did have personality changes that maybe could be overlooked in other people but I hated to see it in my mother. Actually she was no different than a lot of people who drink in that she became argumentative and I soon learned it was useless to try to reason with her then. Nothing was gained and it was best to leave her alone for the most part. I knew she preferred it that way too.

We did try to help her but finally realized that only Mom could make the decision to stop drinking. How ironic that this lovely person who devoted her life to helping others, wasn't able to help herself.

Mom died in the Spring, suddenly of a stroke, but not without warning. She made light of the doctors orders to take it easy, no lifting, special diet, special medicine. But I knew it was serious because she was doing what the doctor said.

It was a sad time for all of us and awful to see my Dad alone after all those years of tender loving care. So it wasn't much of a surprise when he told us he planned to remarry and did by the following September. It was almost unreal to me to lose my mother and have a replacement so soon. But some men just aren't meant to live alone.

So that Fall, the first birthday I had after my Mom died, I felt the urge to go back to my folks house as I usually had. I knew Mom was gone of course, but some how that made me feel the need to see my Dad even more. A childish whim, maybe, but it was an emotional time for me. I made a phone call and Dad said he might have to be gone on business. I told him we'd make the trip anyway because I wanted to see the Fall leaves (Well, that was partly true).

We had a nice drive down, the autumn leaves were exceptionally beautiful. We pulled into the driveway of their house and I could tell no one was home even before we knocked on the door. There was a lot that wasn't there any more. I expected the flower beds to be bare but not be gone completely. The rose beds were gone and so were the many other flower beds my Mom had enjoyed caring for. I guess I could sort of remember Dad saying something about ''the flowers being too much trouble'' but I didn't expect it to look like this.

We knocked on the door, although we knew no one was home. I couldn't help but notice thru the window in the door, the new red carpet and velvet drapes. The dining room was bare, waiting for the new furniture. Yes, I guess his bride had mentioned they were getting new furniture.

I felt sick at my stomach and I knew from the looks on their faces that the rest of my family was feeling the same sadness I was. The person we really wanted to see was indeed gone. Not a word was said but she was in our thoughts every minute. We walked around the yard a little, stretching our legs before the ride back home.

As we walked back to the car, very quietly, not talking much, we walked past a trash can. It was only by chance that I noticed and I couldn't believe my eyes when I saw the delicate little, bisque figurene planter I had given my Mom so many years ago. It was the figure of a young peasant girl sitting sideways on a donkey that was pulling a flower cart. It was so pretty and delicate that I knew Mom would like it so I had to get it for her. She had always kept the planter on the kitchen window sill above the sink and that had been its permanent spot until now. I reached down to pick the figurene up out of the trash, expecting it to fall apart from the way it looked, so lopsided, like it had been tossed with no thought or care about its breaking.

But the figurene seemed to be in one piece and I instinctively looked it over for damage. The only damage I could see was a tiny chip on the girls foot. I could smile at that! I had found a treasure and the trip had a purpose after all.

Now the young girl with the flower cart sits in my window sill and reminds me of the great lady that once enjoyed looking at her!

OCTOBER 19

I've been thinking about that line for a poem
and have come up with a draft. I'm not particularly
pleased with it at the moment but I think it has the
makings of a poem.

Every Woman

Every woman should have a lover who leaves no traces

Who arrives at 9:20
And leaves at 11:20

Whose tastes are simple
Once on top, once on the bottom

Who offers no secrets but his flesh
And sees no mysteries but hers

Who gives used gifts requiring no display
And understands a bargain made of silence

Who puts down the toilet seat
And helps her make the bed

Every woman should have a lover who leaves no traces
Except, of course, they always do.

I think that there is some substance in the poem
as it is now, but much of it is too facile and neat.
In other words, the words and phrases sound smooth
and balanced but I'm not sure they say anything. I'm
especially bothered by the two middle couplets, from
''Who offers'' to ''silence.'' Part of the problem
of writing is that it is hard to give up any words
you put on paper. But writing is not just putting
words on paper and then enshrining them. Good
writing demands that a writer be willing to go over
and over and change and throw out things that won't
communicate. It's all well and good if I as a writer
understand what I mean, but I have to assemble my
words so some readers know what I'm talking about
too.

Writing is a very frustrating business. So what
else is new? I spent all morning playing with
''Every Woman'' and have thrown out the last two
lines and replaced them with these:

Who dresses quietly
And leaves while she's combing her hair.

The change alters the direction of the poem but
it's much more concrete and maybe says something
that's more consistent with the rest of the poem. Oh
well, enough of ''Every Woman;'' maybe tomorrow it
will come together for me.

Chapter X

A few years ago I went into class all giggly and pleased. I guess I showed how I felt because one of my students finally asked what was up. I answered immediately, "My wife just got a job." The class, of course, went wild; they thought that was the funniest thing they'd ever heard.

I realized that I had miscommunicated. Here's the background: for over a year my wife worked at a large local department store as a clerk in basement infants' wear, a job she hated. First of all, she disliked taking the brunt of the customers' wrath; every time a customer was cheated by the store's overpricing of low-quality goods, s/he would be back screaming at her. Second, she really hated being forced to be an accomplice to thievery in the store: she was several times required to remove a tag saying $1.98 and replace it with one saying $3.98. Then she would have to cross out the $3.98 and write $2.98. The tag would finally look like this [3.98̶ / 2.98] so the customer would think it was a dollar bargain when actually it was a cheat, a dollar overcharge. To be sure that clerks would not tell anybody this, the store has a team of spies— "shoppers" they are called. They pretend to be customers and see if the clerks try to cheat them; if they don't, the clerk gets a bad report; too many bad reports and out goes the clerk.

Aside from these problems, the hours were outrageous: she had to work nights and Saturdays and besides that the pay was indecently low—barely above the minimum wage law standard.

Finally one day she got fed up and went out to find a new job. After her interview, I had to go to school; she and I were both hoping like crazy that she'd get the job, but both of us were trying not to get too cocky about it so we wouldn't be disappointed if she didn't get it.

Just before I went from my office to class, I called her. She was shouting and laughing—she had got the job. As a result, when I went into class, I was just as excited.

Now, clearly I didn't communicate to my class when they asked me why I was crazier than usual. When I said, "My wife just got a job," I certainly didn't lie, did I? No, in fact I didn't even stretch the truth. When the class laughed, I could have said to myself, "What a bunch of stupid people—they can't tell the difference between happy news and a joke," Or I could have said, "What are they laughing about? Oh well," And then gone on with the regular business of the class. But I didn't and neither would you.

From their reaction, I knew that—no matter whose fault, mine or theirs—they had not understood what I had tried to communicate. And since at the moment I wasn't in the business of figuring out and placing blame, I explained myself. That's what I usually do—unless I'm writing. But before we look to see what the special problem is with writing let's look to see what happened with my communication.

Words, like a good many other things, are like icebergs—⅞ (was that the figure my teachers used to tell me?) of the meaning under water and only ⅛ of the meaning is visible to everybody. Many times, indeed, the part that is visible ("My wife just got a job") is not even understandable unless the submerged part is exposed.

Look at "My wife just got a job," as one word—a single notion with a sound which hopefully signals "meaning." Everybody who heard the communication knew that my wife is the woman who married me; they knew that a job is something one does for someone else in exchange for money. But they didn't know what I "meant." It was like the iceberg.

_____"my wife got a job"

_____what "my wife just got a job" means

Remember that the waves which separate the viewer from the submerged meaning are constantly moving and shifting—there is no neat line between the visible and submerged parts of the meaning. As a matter of fact the iceberg is one continuous hunk of meaning; how much of the meaning is visible depends on how much gets exposed. The job of the communicator is to expose as much of the meaning needed to get the job done. That's what I did when I explained what the statement "my wife just got a job" meant. Too many times what we do as communicators, expecially as writers, is to give the reader the visible part of the iceberg and let him figure out what lies below.

An important lesson to learn from my experience that night: I failed to communicate at first, but my listeners saved me by telling me what they thought I said—they laughed, and when I heard them laugh I knew I had to explain more fully.

The thing to remember from this is that as communicators we depend very heavily on the person with whom we're communicating, especially when we're speaking. They help us largely by telling us when we need to say more, when we haven't told enough to get the idea. When we write we don't have this help. The successful writer has developed a sensitivity to his or her reader—a feeling for what the reader would ask if he or she could. The successful writer is one who gives that information without being asked. For example, what would you think if I said that when we write, often all we're doing is filling in blanks. You'd likely wonder what in the world I meant by "filling in the blanks." You might stop and wonder what I was talking about. It's perfectly clear to me what you should have got from what I said; the words mean just what they say. What I've given you is an example of the iceberg problem: I gave you the top part, the label, the words which include all I want to say, but that's not enough; you had to know what I meant; you needed a definition.

Now let's say I had stopped with that line about filling in the blanks. Then let's say I showed it to Angela who said, "I doubt a reader will get it; a reader won't know what 'filling in the blanks' means." I could respond in one of two ways. I could say. "Well, what I wrote is right, isn't it? It's up to the reader to understand." The result would be, of course, that the reader wouldn't understand, but I'd feel satisfied and superior—while being an absolute failure.

The other response I could make to Angela's saying that the reader wouldn't get what I was saying is, "Well, what do I have to put down so s/he will get it?" And then put it down. I could pretend that she didn't know about the bottom of that particular iceberg and I could tell her—I could give her the whole business that I'm about to give you.

We've all taken essay tests. We know how they differ from so-called "objective" tests. In fact, many people would say (and do say) that the difference is that objective tests don't involve writing while essay tests do. I've heard so many times I've been believing it without questioning—it's one of those notions that a guy believes, like foreign cars are hard to get serviced, or you have to kick the tires of a used car before you buy it, or people who do bad things should get punished and then they'll be better in the future.

Like those superstitions, the idea that "essay tests are superior because a student has to write" needs some close looking at, but for the moment I'd like to look at the two types of tests from a slightly different angle—I believe they are really similar kinds of writing, very nearly the same, in fact. In neither one are you interested in *communicating* what you're saying. You're simply interested in getting down on paper the appropriate words, sets of lines, "correct" answers. What I'm driving at is a distinction between a communicating consciousness and a fill-in-the-blanks consciousness.

If you wanted to communicate—put an idea of yours into somebody else's head—you probably wouldn't write the message to somebody who already knows that you're saying, somebody who already understands the idea. I never go running up to friends and say "Two and two is four," or "Christopher Columbus came to this continent in 1492." If I did, they would stand there, looking at me, and wait for me to finish. They'd expect me to say more because they expect a person who's tallking to them to say things they haven't heard before.

But writing answers to essay test questions is writing information which the reader already knows—in fact, s/he usually knows it better than the poor stiff who's doing the writing: therefore writing this kind of stuff is not meant to communicate. Oh, all right. It is meant to communicate—but not what the words mean. When we, for example, say on one of these tests "The Civil War was fought for economic reasons," what we are really trying to communicate is "See, Professor Smith, I remember that the war was fought for reasons other than slavery—(and here's the important communication)—just like you said in class and like it said in the book and so you can see how well I pay attention, how carefully I did the assigned reading, and how well I studied." The important message has to do with the writer and his knowledge and study habits—it has little to do with the Civil War.

 ACTIVITY: To understand this idea more clearly, look up the last essay test you took. Write a letter to your brother or sister or friend explaining the concept your teacher had you writing about on the test. For example if the question was "Discuss the concept of self-fulfilling prophecy," write about that idea for your friend instead of for your teacher. Then compare the two versions to see the difference between what I call writing to perform and writing to communicate.

Probably the essay you wrote for the "test" was just another way of filling in the blanks, even though there were no little blank spaces to fill in. You were trying to put down words that *included* what you meant to say—your main concern was whether or not what you wrote *said* what you had in your head. When you tried to get the other person to understand, you were trying to communicate.

Remember what I said before? "You'll be writing to communicate, not simply to fill in the blanks." When I first wrote that, you probably had at best a fuzzy notion of what I was talking about. You knew what the words meant— in a way. You knew what "writing" was and you knew what "filling in the blanks" means. So on one level you could say you knew what the words meant. But for you to understand what I meant. I had to explain myself. Back to the iceberg . . .

"Now and then when we're writing, all we do is fill in the blanks." (pp. 74–75)

All the pages that follow, even this page and the words you're reading now.

Now, I think this kind of consciousness—that the point of writing is to communicate, not just to get the "right" words down; to get the reader to understand what you have in mind, not just put the message in words that include what you mean to say—is basic to becoming a successful writer. The guy who exposes the underwater part of the iceberg has a better chance of getting his message into his reader's head than the guy who simply lays out the top of the iceberg.

If you find yourself asking—"Do these words include what I want them to?"—STOP. Ask yourself instead—"Would I understand this if I were the reader who has no idea of what I'm talking about?"

One more activity to help develop that consciousness:

(1) Break into groups of four or five. Each person tell the others what they'd do on vacation if they had unlimited amounts of money. Everybody write notes while one person is talking.

(2) After the speaker is finished, discuss what he said. Be sure to cover everything he said. Make sure everything is perfectly clear.

(3) Once everybody has had a chance to talk about their vacation, let each person write. Include as much as you can of what you communicated while talking.

(4) Exhcange papers so that everybody sees everbody else's paper. Let the writer know when they didn't include something on paper which he included when talking.

(5) Decide if you need another activity like this. If you do, follow steps one through four, but with a new subject. Try to get the others to understand about one of the nicest sights you've ever seen. (In the country? from the top of a building? a new car? standing at the bottom of a tall building looking up?) Keep doing these activities with new subjects until you're satisfied that you are developing a communicating consciousness as opposed to a fill-in-the-blanks consciousness.

OCTOBER 24

A very quiet girl named Judy Uhrig has been attending the class all semester (I don't think she's missed a class), but she seldom talks out in class. A few days ago she gave me a little piece that she had written called ''My Dog,'' in which she had jotted down some thoughts she had about an experience, or, really, a time in her life. Here is the piece:

My Dog

When I lived in New Mexico I acquired a dog. The mother was just a stray who had pups under a house. The father was said to be a large dog, possibly a wolf.

My puppy was so very chubby it was like a balloon and when it walked it looked like it was crawling.

When I took it out, it always went to the flower beds to play. This and the fact that I was extremely homesick for St. Louis and my mother (who has a flower shop) is the reason I named my puppy ''Flower.''

I loved Flower because really when I played with her it was the same as being in my own back yard again. When Jerry was at work and I took Flower into the meadows to pick wild flowers it was a thing that gave me peace. When I taught Flower tricks, I was really play acting, teaching the fetus that was growing in my womb. I spent the summer in a semi-make-believe world. When I came home in September there was a job for me at Bell Telephone and the objections ''she digs holes,'' ''she'll bite,'' ''she's vicious,'' ''she was too much for me'' and a ''pen'' resulted. I had no time to pet and play with her. I was living back in the rushed world of reality. Then the baby came. Flower was jealous and unhappy. She had to be tied inside the pen to prevent getting loose and the howling was awful sad.

Finally a move to another house but also a move to a smaller pen shared by another dog already meek from loss of life. Flower's spirit broke, she became a vegetable. It hurt but I lied to myself and kept saying ''some-day.''

Then one morning she lost her mind and in 12 hours her movability and then she died having convulsions.

I loved her like no other dog and now I find I despise all other dogs. I am afraid of them and for them until the time of ''some-day.''

This is a note Judy wrote when she handed me the ''complete'' version:

''The first time I wrote this it was very painful but while recopying I acquired the ability to control my emotions and look at it over all and I realize it is far from good. I still have a lot inside me I haven't said yet. I'm going to keep at it.''

Today Judy came by my office with a new version of her piece. We had been talking about moving from ''filling-in-the-blanks'' to communicating. And while the first version may have been clear to her, I think in this version she is able to uncover the whole of Dick's iceberg. She shows concern for her reader: here is the rewrite she brought me:

My Dog

My life is like a fast moving stream that gathers life as it flows down the mountain side. Have you ever tried to stop a stream by putting your hand there? All that happens is that your hand forms a small dam and the water rises and goes over the top. My life is the same as that stream when I try to cut a slice out of my life and tell it to some one it is like the stream. You can't just take it as it is, you have to get a little more and a little less along with what I really wanted to tell so bear with me and I will reveal all of me in the naked truth that exposes life.

An eternity ago I lived in the mountains of New Mexico. It was a heavenly place. We camped on the top of a mountain. The days were perfect

except for the rain or hail that came each day
between twelve and two. The nights were
delightfully cold. The little clearing was such
a primitive green and it was lined with little
trees that were individually formed but looked
all alike to me. The water in the six inch wide
stream was always like ice.

The men would leave each day to cut the tall
trees and I alone would be in camp. I was always
afraid and at the same time awed. There were
never any humans around to disturb me and I
usually just sat around rolling my own
cigarettes, which usually fell apart, and trying
to organize everything a little better. I could
put fear at the back of my mind because it was
so peaceful except when my clearing was invaded
by wild horses I had to climb trees ""to be
safe'' or when I would hear the howling away off
that would send shivers up my back.

It was in this world that I had my first
clue that I was pregnant. I couldn't have been
over two weeks pregnant when I received a
terrific pain in my womb. I realized then that I
was to be a mother.

We were only in the mountains for one week,
then we moved to town for the next couple weeks.
It was a crazy town. The name was Eagle Nest.
All it contained was hotels and a lake.

We weren't making it, so here I took on my
first job, as a cleaning lady. That was such a
laugh. Me a cleaning lady, me, who never mopped
in my life or even knew how to make a bed
properly. But thru the kindness of the two
Mexican ladies I was to help, they taught me how
and covered up my mistakes. Like the time I
tried to iron the table cloths and burned them
all. They showed me such kindness and favored me
quite a bit. They used to bring me little things
in their lunch. It was fruit or a sandwich, once
they gave me something that was a cross between
a peach and an apple, or so they said. It was
sure delicious. Their language was very broken

so our conversations were limited but a smile can reveal so much. It's funny, I worked there almost the full week and was supposed to get a whole two dollars a day, but we left without even collecting it. I didn't get to frame the first dollar I ever made.

It was while I was here in Eagle Nest that I found Flower. We went to visit some friends of Jerry's who lived in a trailer where we had left our car that had a flat. Under another ladie's log cabin there was a sad old she dog. She was all bones and white as a ghost. She had a litter of the fattest eight pups I had ever seen.

They were just ripe for being taken away. All that were left were females but I have always had a symbolic closeness to underdogs of any kind. Female dogs falling into that category. She was the prettiest pup. All round and fluffy and soft. Her fur was a peachy tan, a color I've never seen before or since.

One day she was competing for a bowl of gravy with the rest of the dogs nearby when I heard her yelp and come rushing to me. Like a hurt child she looked into my face and seemed to say. ""The bully hit me.'' Her ear was completely covered with white milk gravy. It was so funny but from then on I knew she would be more than just another dog. Dogs I had had all my life since I could remember. They were those stupid creatures we kept around to look at now and then but this one would be different. She would be like a child for me to love and teach things to. She had to have a special name, Spot or Rover just wouldn't do or any name like poor GTO, that was named that way because I happened to be crazy about that car at the time. Her name had to be special because she was a special thing to me. I searched my mind between all the shadows but nothing would come out. I started to become more homesick each day. At least there I'd get a free meal. I started writing to Mom. I knew she ""really'' didn't love me or she

wouldn't have acted the way she always did and
kept my feet glued where they were for if she
didn't love me then I certainly wouldn't waste
time loving her and her ""stupid'' flower shop.

One afternoon I let Flower out and like all
days before she headed straight for the flower
beds but today she seemed to want to be a
flower. As soon as I thought it, I knew that was
the lovely name for her because the beauty and
love for her would be like unto a beautiful
flower.

Jerry was like all men that I knew. Afraid
of being called a sissy, yet not man enough to
do what he really wanted to do. He was, as you
called it, ""Programmed Very Well.'' He
pretended to dislike Flower but I knew better.
There were times I had caught him playing with
her when he thought no one was around. She had
captured even him.

We moved not long after that to Chama. Chama
was more like a little city. The first day we
were there they had a nice little parade. All
the stores in town had an elaborate float. They
even threw candy to all the children. There were
more people and more life. We finally got our
first house there. It was worse than any ghetto
I had ever seen but it was beautiful because we
didn't have to share it with anyone else. I was
the mistress of the house.

Flower developed into that really cute stage
there. I started having morning sickness then,
only it just wasn't only in the morning, it was
every time I ate no matter when. I remember it
was as regular as eating. After I ate I'd go to
the restroom like most people do, to brush their
teeth, only I had a different reason. We had
enough food in those days but I then had the
trials of learning to cook. I remember the first
meal I cooked, fried chicken, mashed potatoes
and gravy. The chicken was burnt on the outside
and raw on the inside. The potatoes were lumpy
and had too much butter and they were syrupy.

The gravy was worst of all. We had gravy at home
all the time and I knew what went in it but not
how much. I kept waiting for it to turn brown
and thicken. I must have added a half gallon of
milk and two cups of flour. Needless to say how
it ended up. I was terribly upset when Jerry
wouldn't eat it. Making tortillas was even
worse. The Mexican lady I asked must have
thought I meant pancakes. Flower wouldn't even
eat the mistakes. She ate just about everything
else, vegetables, breads, even lettuce. I
finally mastered french fries and fried eggs.

The days were lonely because again I was
alone but spent my time doing my newly found
skills. Cleaning and scrubbing and I even
started a quilt which is still not done.

I always found time to take Flower over to
the meadow to play while I picked my wild
flowers. Wild flowers are also in the underdog
category because they grow all by their self. I
used to pick all the different kinds. There were
so many colors, yellow, blue, pink and white.
And some had very intricate leaves that I picked
for fern. I'd take them home and arrange them in
glasses and cans that I got out of the dump not
far away. I had them all over the house. When I
did this I felt peace because it was like at
home, working with flowers. While I picked
flowers, Flower could smell and jump and run and
find the funniest ways to entertain me. When she
wandered too far I used to whistle and she'd
come back. She had a fascination for rocks and
would dig them around like a pig. She developed
her hunting skill about that time then too. We
had a skunk who lived under our house and she
once went in after it and wouldn't come out.
That night I called and called her but she
wouldn't come out. We went on to bed but I
couldn't sleep because I was so afraid for her
and too afraid of the dark to go out and make
her come in. I woke Jerry who was really too
tired to be disturbed and asked him to go and

get her. He objected because no harm would behold her, I was afraid for no reason. I threw a terrible temper tantrum and cried hysterically. He went and got Flower.

I cried a lot those days. I was more emotional in everything. I craved something more. I had a funny little blindness every time I got up from lying or sitting. I even had a true black out. I remember I was walking past the bathroom thinking about an old girl friend. My mind didn't alter its course but my facilities did. I realized I was sitting on the floor still thinking about Eva. It was an extraordinary feeling.

My days became boring and I wanted to read something. I went to our landlord's house to borrow her Bible because while I was in the mountains I had started reading it then. I made it thru Matthew, Mark, Luke and John. The lady though didn't have a Bible, all she had was the book of Mormon. I wasn't particular so I borrowed it. I read the first one hundred and fifty pages and had to know more. She introduced me to the two Mormon missionaries who came and gave me the six lessons about their faith. I believed. I knew it was the truth. The people are the ones who really convinced me. Especially the men. The missionaries, who were only boys of twenty, were more of a man than any I had ever seen. They matched more with my dream of what men really should be. The women too, they seemed to drink water from a fountain of goodness. They weren't acting faky or even pushed their character. They really wanted to be what they were. Mothers and Wives. I repented, even quit smoking cigarettes while Jerry flaunted his stubborness to accept. He was totally absorbed in jealousy of the missionaries. He didn't have the nerve to tell me I couldn't bring them to the house, he merely pretended they weren't there.

Our first fight was really a blow. I was
tired of everything and wanted to go for a drive
alone. Jerry was afraid I'd leave him and
insisted he go with me. The whole purpose of
going for a drive was to get away from him. I
tried to explain this to him but he wouldn't
budge. He placed himself behind the wheel which
infuriated me. I began to beat his back and when
he turned around to protest I attacked his face
with all the fury of a blizzard. Blood gushed
from his mouth, nose and cheeks. He was so
startled not to mention how I felt. I had never
felt such anger for any thing or any one before.
He just got out and went inside. I left. I came
home hours later with a terrible guilt complex.
He was so glad I had returned that he wasn't mad
any more.

A date was set for my baptism and there were
many shadows over my face. My mother called and
pleaded with me to come home. I agreed. She
would send me the money. Jerry didn't want me
to. He cried and I developed a harshness which
is in me yet for crying men. We agreed that I'd
drop him off at his home in Arkansas. Meanwhile
we waited. I packed my clothes and he his. We
would walk to the Post Office one and one half
miles away each way.

Once on the way to the Post Office there was
a car that threw out a baby kitten behind us. As
I tried to retrieve it, the kitten became
frightened and ran under the wheels of a large
truck waiting to turn left. The men stopped and
I crawled under the truck to get the kitten. I
was awfully afraid the kitten would be killed if
I didn't get it and at the same time I was
afraid the men would start up again with me
under there. Flower was in my arms and she was a
handful alone. As I neared the kitten, she
lunged also and there was a lot of spitting and
scratching in my hands. We all made it to safety
but Jerry wouldn't help me control the two

little creatures. The kitten was named Faith and she cried the next twenty four hours.

A few days later we heard a car drive up. I went to see who it was. It was my sister and brother. I was shocked. Instead of sending me money she sent me relatives. They were nice and we made the trip home non-stop in twenty hours. Flower, Faith, me and whoever was inside me making me sick all the time.

When we got home I stayed with my mother. She had a nice large fenced in yard where Flower could romp and roam and still be safe. There is a thing in my family about dogs in the house. The few weeks I stayed here contained detailed job hunting. I searched every where possible. I finally got my job at Bell Telephone as a long distance operator. The job was good but the hours horrible. They were different almost every day. My favorite hours were a split shift, one to four in the afternoon and eight to eleven at night. These were great because after I got off work I still had a couple of hours to roam the taverns that I had become accustomed to going to and I didn't have to be at work until one the next day so it gave me time to recuperate. Flower started digging holes. My sister and her husband had separated so she asked me to move in with her, which was right behind my mother's house, so I did. Her yard wasn't fenced but there was a dog pen in it. It was about twenty feet long and six feet wide. Flower didn't like the pen but she didn't have a choice. With all my gallivanting around, the only time I saw Flower was once a day when I fed and watered her. I started treating her like all the rest of the dogs I had had, because now it wasn't just her and me all day long, it was me and all these scads of people I had to please. I had put myself in a very awkward position but I didn't realize it then. I just kept on trying to please them.

I quit working when I was eight months
pregnant. The morning sickness had left off at
three months, and I could feel it kicking at
five months. I had no real pains to mention any
more.

I learned to jitter bug and sort of settled
back to be a mother. While I was off work I
started on my quilt again and knitted a little.
I even snuck Flower in the house a couple of
times but she was so glad that she acted wild.
Running around smelling everything at top speed.
She wasn't a little pup any more either, she
weighed at least seventy five pounds now. And on
her journey thru the house what she didn't break
she knocked over. I realized that she could no
longer be an inside dog so we played outside a
few times but I wasn't an outside person then,
so we went back to seeing each other only once a
day. Flower was the picture of health though.
She was that beautiful undescribable color.

She was marked with a little black on her
back like a husky. Her hair was extremely thick,
short, straight, and coarse. Her eyes were
really noticeable, they were outlined in black
just like she had eye liner on and big brown
eyes. She became extremely vicious and a good
watch dog. She'd bark at the slightest noise and
act as if she was trying to tear the pen down if
anyone came about. She was very fierce looking
when she wanted to be. She'd bare her teeth and
had a special sound she'd make. The hair on her
head and back would stand on end. Her eyes would
shoot sparks.

My baby came in the spring, March 29th to be
exact. I brought the baby home. His name was
Douglas Randolph. I was so amazed that I could
produce such a beautiful and perfect little
being that I held him almost day and night.
During the day we'd sit in the yard. Flower was
extremely jealous of the baby and would whine
and act so pitiful. After she knew the baby was

there at night sometimes she'd be so unhappy
that she'd howl for hours. It was always a low,
mournful howl that always made me cry.

When Douglas was almost three months old my
sister and I got into an argument and I went
back to my mother's. This time however they made
a pen for Flower which was very small. And threw
in poor old GTO who was already meek from loss
of life. About this time I'd become baptised and
Doug was blessed. Flower soon had puppies. So
did GTO within three days of each other. Flower
had hers first, seven of them, G had eight.
Flower was a very good mother. I was proud of
her. I think the mark of a good dog is how good
a mother she is. In fact after G had pups Flower
used to go and steal a few of G's thinking they
were hers.

During one of these stealing episodes G
killed one dog, two others died because G
wouldn't let them nurse. That left a total of
twelve dogs. We gave each mother six. Flower was
a very good and conscientious mother. She took
G's puppies and did very well. G however was not
so good, she killed two more of her pups.

Flower became thinner but we fattened her
back up. But after we took her pups away she
became meek and mild. She no longer barked like
she used to. She didn't howl either. She didn't
dig holes but she did climb. We had a four foot
fence around the dog pen which she had no
trouble at all going over so we increased it
another four foot but she still managed to go
over but not as frequently. My mother disliked
Flower because she brought back memories of the
past, decided that we should chain Flower inside
the pen thereby eliminating her climbing out. We
did.

One day when I went to feed Flower she was
acting awfully funny. She would start to walk
and when she'd walk her limit, to the fence,
she'd keep on walking. Like a toy truck run by
battery. It only goes so far until something

gets in the way. It keeps going on and on until you turn it around and let it go the other way. It was awful pitiful, she had that glazed look in her eye. But I had no time, I had to rush to work or I'd be late, the boss mad and maybe get fired. I'd look at her at night.

That evening she no longer could walk. She'd lay and pant. No control over her muscles. Her body was covered with mud and caked on dirt. She smelled rotten, flies already covered her eyes, nose, and mouth. She had upset her water and looked as if she had rolled in the dirt. We fed her raw eggs and milk. It seemed to relax her. We eliminated the flies with a spray. She rested.

That night she started having convulsions, fits, foaming at the mouth. Great agony and pain, she no longer was my beloved little child or even a lowly dog. She had become a worm, twisting, writhing and turning on a hook. Silent and screaming pain. She died.

Her life was terribly bad. She had lost out. Love, gentleness and warmth she had had so little. Her death was a final suffering. I buried her in a ditch. Her bones are long bare and her coat is rotted away but she lives in my heart. The mere thought of her brings back all these memories and more. They will never die. The fear I have of dogs now is very cruel. I fear they will take a warm place in my heart like Flower and receive only the cruel harshness of a world yet not ready to accept a body or person, unable to turn her back on the world like that summer in New Mexico. Someday things may change. They always do and are fast doing so. I will hold on to my hope of some day and content my self with that until some day happens.

Chapter XI

Another aspect of communication which is important here is called non-verbal communication. It has to do with all that information we deliver without words when we talk.

For example, notice that when you're talking to some one and your listener doesn't understand, s/he usually says so without words. A grunt or a "huh?" or just an expression on their face does the job.

As a matter of fact, we do a lot of communicating without words. It isn't just a matter of facial expressions, either. For example, many times much of what we have to say gets supplied by how close we stand to the listener—to see this in operation, try the following:

 Break the class into pairs. Take turns saying "Nice day today, isn't it?" Say it from a distance of about five feet. Next say the same thing from a distance of one foot. Be careful to say it the same way; don't change your expression. (If you smiled or giggled the first time, smile or giggle the second time.) Don't do anything different—just be closer.

In our culture, we seem to carry about with us some two feet of space; we're standing in the middle of a circle two feet in diameter. This space belongs to us and we will not have it invaded except for special purposes, usually sexual or aggressive. (Are these two sides of the same coin?) For example, have you ever noticed how uncomfortable most people are in an elevator? And, in a doctor's office, if there's a whole room full of empty chairs with one person sitting there, don't we usually sit away from that person? The same thing goes on the bus.

 Here's an interesting experiment: Next time you're at a party talking to one person, keep moving closer. If the other person starts to back away, keep moving closer. Be careful though: don't be too obvious; just pretend you don't even notice that you are standing so close.

Ask the following questions out loud, being sure to watch what happens to your voice on the last word.

(1) Where are you going tonight?

(2) Do you like that restaurant?

(3) What do they have to eat there?

(4) Are omelets the specialty of the house?

(5) What kind of omelets do you like best?

(6) Are you noticing that all these questions have to do with eating?

(7) What do you think I'm thinking about now?

(8) Did you guess I'm hungry?

What all this means is that you say more with questions than just what the words mean. When you let your voice move up in "Are you going to the show or restaurant?" you are telling the listener to answer "yes" or "no." When you send your voice down on "tonight" you are saying "I know you are going to one or the other; I just want to know which one."

Well this is all very interesting, but what does it all mean? Two important lessons:

(1) You've been using skills like raising your voice all through your life—well, almost all through it; nobody took you aside and said, "when you want to get a yes-or-no answer, you should raise your voice." You heard people doing it and you learned to communicate this way just as you learned the other aspects of your language. Now when somebody asks you at a party "Would you like beer, wine, or vodka?" you can intentionally misunderstand the question and pretend that they sent their voice up on vodka. You can confuse them by answering "Yes." And since they know that that isn't the response they told you to give, they'll get the joke too. Lesson one: you know a whole lot more than you know you know, you have an ability that you use without being conscious of using it. It's an almost unconscious talent—the trick for a writer is to use it consciously, to know *all* the information they want to send out when talking, not just the information included in the words. Which leads to another important idea:

(2) A lot of this nearly instinctive communication is done without words. You send your voice up and it doesn't just mean "?"; it sends out a whole lot more information. And it isn't just a matter of questions either.

 Choose an innocent sound like your name. Say it as many ways as you can and discuss what information you give in addition to the sound of your name. "Larry" (come home). "Larry" (watch out for the truck). "Larry" (I'm warning you: do that again and I'll

. . .), "Larry" (How do you do), "Larry" (You sure your name isn't Harriet?), "Larry" (Come help me), "Larry" (What a nasty thing to say), "Larry" (What a nasty thing to say, but I think it's funny), "Larry" (Oh, thank you for the nice present). And these are just a few examples; maybe you can think of others.

Tell someone to "come home now," saying it in as many different ways as you can—be sexy, angry, gentle, tough, and so on. Discuss what the extra meanings were.

All this has to do with another one of the difficulties of successful communication in writing. A lot of people tell me things like "Writing and speaking are two different systems." For example, writing, they say, is in whole sentences, while speaking isn't necessarily that formal. Now that kind of talk is sort of interesting if you're interested in that sort of thing (which I am) but it doesn't get people very far when they're trying to translate what they could easily say into lines on paper—that is, when they're trying to communicate what would be easy if they were talking, but seems impossible in writing. Besides, I'm not so sure it's true to say that we have two different systems—but I suppose that it all depends on how you define "system" and "different." Anyway, I write and speak without sentences, but I really don't think about it all that much.

To me the big difficulty in moving from talking to writing is that the writer has to be aware of all the information s/he provides without words, and since s/he can't raise his or her voice or wave his or her hand or move closer to the listener, s/he has to figure out some way to get all that information down on paper. In short, writing needs more words than talking does. Once you are aware of the information you'd be giving your listener with gestures, facial expressions, and moving your voice around, then you have to get that information into words.

 Now, using only the paper and pencil, find words to tell each other to come home now, but with all the different additional information you were sending before with your faces, voices, hands, etc.

Compare papers with others in the class—which papers seem to get the message across? Why? Which ones seem most interesting? Why?

(1) Write a letter to a friend telling about some game or activity you think is fun or exciting. Tell about something you really like to do. Eat? Fix cars? Play Monopoly? Sleep? Swim? Dance? When you've finsihed the letter get back into groups of 3

or 4 and read what you've written to each other. Only what is written down, nothing else. If you feel a need to add something, too bad this time. What will be happening, if you feel this need, is that your instincts are telling you that more information is needed. Well, maybe it isn't your "instincts" alone. Maybe your listeners are telling you—by hardly noticeable signals—that they want to know more; they're saying "I don't completely understand; tell me more about it." If you should get this feeling, make a mark where you wanted to add something.

(2) Later today, write the thing over until you're satisfied that you've included everything you want to.

OCTOBER 26

I was visiting friends who live in Springfield, Illinois recently. Deb and Harry are my age and their daughter Leah is three. Leah is a talkative child with a young child's disarming directness. When I used a toothpick after a messy encounter with corn on the cob, she informed me ''We use those for our olives when my Poppa makes martinis.

I'm drifting away from the point of my story. Leah was eating cherries and had smeared her face and hands with the juice. Deb suggested that Leah might want to wash up. A few minutes later Leah returned displaying her clean hands and once again white chin. ''See, I'm clean now,'' she announced. I answered ''That's a lot better than having red yucko all over yourself, isn't it?''

Leah nodded. But Deb, being both motherly and precise, turned to Leah, said, ''That's cherry juice.''

Which only goes to prove that one woman's ''red yucko'' is another woman's ''cherry juice.''

I could argue about which of us was more exact (I think Deb wins) or more picturesque (I vote for me), but that's not the point I'm interested in here. We each said what we said because our goals in speaking were different and our visions of what was happening in the situation were different.

Deb wants Leah to develop her language skills by
learning the correct words for anything she's
interested in. I am in the midst of a several week
love affair with the word ''yucko.'' I enjoy saying
it. The sound pleases me. The fact that it is an
adolescent slang word entertains my sort-of-grown-up
mind. And plain and simple, it's been a while since
I've encountered a new word with such a strong
visceral image. In other words, it sounds to me
sticky, messy, and childlike. ''Yucko'' is when my
ice cream cone drips all over my hands. ''Yucko'' is
melted bubble gum on the sole of my shoe at the ball
park. ''Yucko'' is a kid's mess and I love it.
''Yucko'' is strawberry-flavored sugarless bubble
gum and Hostess Chocodiles—both of which I smuggle
into my house amid the scoffs of my friends who
contend that no one could like that junk.

What I'm saying is that the right word is the
business of the writer or speaker, who, we hope,
knows what he or she is talking about. That is, I
may drink some cherry juice this evening but if I
spill it on my blouse it will become ''red yucko''
and no one can tell me differently.

OCTOBER 28

From Kevin Friel's journal:

                                    so many

                there

                 he sits

                in his corner

                  thinking

        why   of life

                  as he is

                  looking

```
                with

                 in

               a mirror

            drinking

              a tear

          seen without

          for

          so few words

                never to pass

          'n a smile

               beyond beginning

          lost

            as life is

          trembling

                alone

          iri

               kevin d. friel
```

NOVEMBER 3

   Last Monday night, I was having conferences for
an hour and a half before my 8:30 class. As I sat
talking to the students who had appointments to see
me, I became more and more conscious of the fact
that my throat was getting sorer and sorer. By ten
after eight I was thinking of meeting the class and
sending them home since I had developed a headache
too. When I get the flu, it starts out with a sore
throat and headache and I end up stuck in bed with
aches and pains and barely enough energy to watch my
favorite soap operas so I was not looking forward to
the next few days.

My last appointment was with Richard Putney who
took one look at me and said, ''You're sick.''

I told him that I was thinking of letting the
class go and he said, ''I've got something I'd like
to read in class tonight. Then we can go home and it
won't be like everybody stayed out here for
nothing.''

''Okay,'' I said, happy to have a way out of
doing anything that required any thought or energy
and pleased that I wouldn't have to feel guilty
about the students who had been waiting around for
an hour or who had come to school for my class only.

When we got to class, Richard read. Then Gary
said he had something sort of like what Richard had
written, so he read. Then Paul said that he wanted
to read too. So I sat there getting sicker and
sicker and wondering how the hell I had succeeded in
teaching this class so that they ran it themselves
even when I wished they'd all go home. I'm sure that
if I had wanted them to take over, class would have
lasted ten or fifteen minutes. Instead, I finally
asked them if they'd mind if I left.

I'm writing this on Friday, I did have the flu,
and I've recovered. And here's what Richard and Gary
and Paul read.

Richard's piece:

One of my earliest and fondest memories is
of fishing. The first time I remember going
fishing was in the summer of 1952 in Anchorage,
Alaska.

There was a river about a mile from our
house called Ship Creek, which fed glacial
waters into Cook Inlet then into the Gulf of
Alaska.

I remember taking my red wagon and fishing
pole and going off alone to fish in the creek
for salmon. You can't imagine the beauty of the
crystal clear water and the sun sparkling on the
sides of silver salmon or the bright red humps
of the humpback or chinook salmon, swimming up-
river to spawn. The fish were so thick you

seldom had to wait more than 2 or 3 minutes to
catch a fish. My limit was 2 because that is all
I could carry at one time. I could carry a
salmon over my shoulder and it's tail would drag
6 inches on the ground. I would spend all
morning there then drag my fish home and clean
them.

While my mother fixed the fish, I would go
outside and play or slip over across the street
and steal strawberries out of a neighbors
garden. Once I had a bucket full, which didn't
take long since they were the size of silver
dollars. I would run home and sit by the faucet
and rinse them and eat them. Rinse, eat, rinse,
eat, etc.; just like an assembly line. I never
did get sick, but after we moved from Alaska I
never had much of an appetite for strawberries
anymore.

One day in 1953 or 1954, I don't remember
the year, I started to go on my little fishing
trip and saw everything looking gray and dusty.
I asked my mother what was happening because
there was no sun, even though it was summer, and
there was dust all over everything. It turned
out that a volcano had erupted some 50 to 60
miles away and what we were seeing was ash.
Seems this volcano was a type that belched ashes
rather than lava. Sort of like blowing into a
pipe from a wood stove that hasn't been cleaned
for a long time. It was an interesting
experience for sure.

Anchorage was a much more interesting place
to live than Adak, which is located in the
Aleutian Islands. We lived on Adak for about 6
months, but the only interesting thing that
happened there, of any consequence, was an
extremely clear day. ''What's exciting about a
clear day?'', you may ask. If all you saw was a
grey rock, grey buildings, and grey days you
would understand why a clear day was exciting.
Anyway, this day happened to be extremely clear
as I said, and with a pair of binoculars I was

able to see across the Bering Strait and see the shores of Siberia. This was really something for a kid of my tender years! Imagine standing in you're own yard looking at a foreign country, and Russia of all places! Remember, the Korean War was closer to Alaska than a newspaper article and our feelings about Russia were still rather guarded from experiences in World War II.

Believe me, experiences like these are not forgotten very easily, and they can never be replaced.

What Gary Jostes read:

The following morning broke clear and crisp as I slipped on my chest waders, gathered my gear and headed for the river. Small mammals scurried away in the predawn stillness while others froze in position to stare unbelievingly. Sliding noiselessly into the icy waters, I scanned the streams' eddys' and pools for rise forms; the tell-tale sign of feeding fish. The splashy taking of surface insects was evident.

An unusually large ring of water rippled outward as a fish sucked an unsuspecting caddie fly from the film.

I pulled thirty yards of line into a false cast, then shot it upstream and across the current. The distance was correct to float the imitation to the feeding fish. I mended line in the rushing water and waited. With three consecutive casts and no strike, I waded upstream.

Fishing the likely holding positions yielded five medium-size steelhead. These sea-run rainbow trout made startling runs and energenic flights. They were released gently after admiring their sleek shiny colors.

Meanwhile the salmon could still be seen leaping in mid current. Finding a spot which would afford maximum backcast, I hurled another ten feet of line in a forward roll cast. Some fish were holding near the bottom and a small hen was fooled by my offering.

Perhaps small by Salmon terms, the eleven pound Chinook made three long fighting rushes which nearly went into the flyline backing. Several minutes of playing finally tired the fish and it was brought to net. It was released and I continued wading.

Spotting a large boulder, I cast into the swirling water behind.

The salmon was laying there, devouring nymphs and insect larvae washed downstream.

With no response to the Quill Gordon, I overturned rocks to discover which species of fly was prevalent.

Switching to a Caddis Pupa, another cast was made after resting the eddy for a few minutes. It was unnerving to keep from setting the hook too early as I saw the fin slicing water. It reminded me of a scene from Jaws where the water parts with spray cascading from a huge dorsal fin.

This was a king indeed!

As I set the hook, aware of the line tension, the salmon went into a head shaking tail walk. It careened downstream at lightning speed, line screaming from my reel. As soon as the thought could register, I headed downstream in pursuit.

The thin tippet would snap if I ran out of line with such a long run. If I could keep up, there would be a chance. The bank was clear behind me so I headed for it. After running out of beach, I waded again, stopping momentarily to fight the monster as it circled, preparing to dash again.

If it would head upstream, the force of the current would be to my advantage. The salmon, usually quartering in the Pacific, only returns to the river in spring and fall to spawn in the headwaters. Many obstacles are overcome during these pilgrimiges, making the king chinook salmon wary and strong.

This fish had learned its lesson well, for it never turned, but continued to hurtle down the channel.

Luck smiled on me however as the demon encountered boulders, and was diverted to a placid side pool. Clearly out of breath and seventy yards behind, I gathered line frantically while navigating the rock strewn terrain.

The salmon was resting as I made my way to the pool's edge. The battle continued as my falling shadow struck terror in the creature's heart. Limited in space, but still full of fight, it twisted and turned in the throes of freedoms passion. The leader pinged dangerously from one rock to the next. Holding the rod tip high, I stood firm only to gain line and then lose it to the maddened fish.

As time wore on, so did the monster; its thrashing becoming more and more feeble. In one final desperate gesture, it leaped and miraculously returned mainstream.

Not wanting to admit defeat after coming so close to victory, I pivoted and hurridly tried to reduce the line slack. The salmon, tired in its blind frustration, swam erroringly upstream. The force of water was too much as it turned on its side and began to drift in the flow. Reaching behind me, I unsnapped the dip net, continuing to maintain a taunt line.

With gentle urgings of the rod, I guided the fish into the rope mesh. Barely inside the rim, it panicked once again nearly escaping.

Too large for the net, I directed it toward shallow water. With fins scraping bottom, the silvery knight of the Rogue River was finally beached.

Exhilleration flooded me as I studied its pinkish orange markings. The Chinook was even more awesome at close confrontation. His twenty one pound bulk would cover my wall amply. Its fleshy sides would satisfy a table full of hungry guests or a small kodiac bear.

The pleasures mother nature has offered us
are numerous. In return all around me man is
trying to destroy the natural and mould it into
his own misguided unchanging structural world.

With my heart in my throat I held the salmon
in the current until the flow of oxygen thru
gills revived it.

With a thankful wag of its tail, it
disappeared into the murky depths.

Wiser now, it would continue to fight
further obstacles until its goal was met.
Perhaps it would survive the ordeal and spawn
many more of its own kind, the only hope against
extinction.

In these changing times we must do all we
can to preserve this natural gift for future
generations. Enjoy with nature, do not take from
it; for once it is gone it can not be returned.

The memory of a battled fish will remain
forever, however a killed fish ends with its
death, killing enjoyable memories which could be
shared by many.

Satisfied I headed for home, my dreams
complete.

Paul Bohler's piece:

The other day I went Goose hunting at Swan
Lake Conservation Reserve. It is near Summer,
Mo. which is approx. 250 miles north west of St.
Louis. We left Saturday about 3:30 pm and drove
for four and one half hours before our arrival
to Swan Lake headquarters building. I went with
three guys I grew up with, Mark, Tom and John.
Mark and Tom are brothers. Well we got to Swan
Lake about 9:00 pm and started getting ready for
bed. Mark's van is what we were in, he has it
all set up for camping. He has a bed for two, it
is all carpeted and he has a stove and heater.
He also has a very nice stereo in it. Once we
got settled we cooked supper, a big pot of stew
with apple cider which we heated with cinnamon

sticks, man it was good. Once we finished eating
we settled down into our sleeping bags. Mark and
Tom were on the bed, I slept under the bed and
John, who is not very tall slept at the foot of
the bed crossway in the van. After all our
fooling around we did not get to bed till 12:30
am. That would not be so bad but reservation
time was at 4:45 am, so we had to get up at 3:00
am. At three am when that alarm went off I felt
like I did not even get to bed. We got up and
dressed and I ran up to the headquarters and got
in line for our blind. See what you do is mail
in to Swan Lake a reservation permit and if you
are lucky enough you get a reservation time and
date. What happens in line is when you get to
the window you give the conservation agent your
reservation card and each man's hunting license.
He checks each one and fills out a card which
shows each man in the blind and the blind
number. The way you get a number is the agent
spins a cage and a ball with a number comes out
and that is your blind number. We got R-3. They
give you a map on how to get to your blind and
off you go. We also rented two dozen decoys.
Once we got to the parking place you have to
carry everything to your blind, your gun,
decoys, we also had a stove that we took so we
could cook a hot lunch, and it helps to keep you
warm. We got to the blind, which was
approximately 175 yards from the road in an old
corn field. The mud was about 1' deep. In the
middle of the field is the blind, or pit as some
people call it. The blind is 8 x 4 and is 5'
deep. It sits about 2' out of the ground and we
covered it with leaves, sticks and high grass in
order to camouflage ourselves. Once this was
done we got into the blind and waited till 6:36
am. Sunup! This is when you can start hunting,
not a minute before. See you hunt from sun-up to
sun-down, which was 6:36 am to 4:52 pm.

We sat for about two and one half hours
until the first geese came over us. The way you

pick your goose depends on where you are in the blind. We were from right to left, Mark, Tom, me, John. There were four geese in the first pass. John would take the first one, I would take the second one, Tom the third and Mark the last one. Just as they got over us and we got up to fire John changed his mind and told me to take the lead one. I fired, dropping the lead goose. He set his wings and glided down rather fast and hit the ground approximately sixty yards away. A shot gun is accurate up to about 50 yards, farther then that is luck. I started to get out of the blind and noticed the goose got up and started looking around. I got very excited and just as I got out of the blind I fell down right in one foot of mud. I was also carrying my gun, luckily it didn't go in the mud. I got up and started running after the goose. First I should tell you what I had on. Two pairs of socks, long-johns, blue-jeans, rubber chest high pants, two coats and hip boots. Now, if you can picture this, here I am running after a goose in one foot of mud with all that on. I ran about one hundred yards, stopped and fired again at the goose, it fell. As I started toward him he got up again and started running. Now he is crossing the road and going toward the refuge wire. Once crossed he is free, I can not cross or shoot into the refuge. I got to the road and stopped, he was about six feet from the wire, he stopped. I was very tired, I had to shoot and get him before he crossed the line. I raised my gun but I was so tired I could not hold it still, I fired, and missed. He ran across the wire to safety, and I stood on the road, tired, muddy and down three shells. That was another thing I forgot to tell you. Each hunter can only take 10 shells with him into the blind. There were four of us so we had forty shells. Once you use your ten, you are done hunting. That keeps guys from sky busting.

That is when you fired a couple into a flock of geese that are too high to hit but you may get lucky anyway and cripple one so he comes down into range.

Once back into the blind we all relaxed and talked about how funny it was to see me fall in the mud and running thru the mud after a goose. It was kind of funny. We sat for about one hour before we got any more good shots, but we missed. Finally about eleven-ten am we spotted three geese coming straight at us, about 35 yards up. This is the hardest shot when the geese come right at you because you have to lead them and coming straight at you it is very difficult. They were a little on my side so John took the lead, I took second and Tom took the third one. Just as we started to get up to shoot John again changed his mind. He said for me to take the lead goose again. So as before I fired and bingo, I downed the goose. Only this time the goose did not get back up. I had my first goose. John also got one but Tom missed his.

We went out and got our geese. As it turned out both were female geese. Mine was 8 lbs. even and John's was 6.5 lbs. We stayed around in the blind for about two more hours. Mark fired all ten of his shells but didn't get a goose. Tom fired nine shells and while we were waiting for more geese it started raining very hard so we called it quits. One other thing about my goose was she had a band on her leg. On the band is a number and an address. What you do is write to the address and give them the number and when and where you got the goose and they send you all the information about the goose.

After we left the blind we had to go back to the headquarters and register our geese and get back our licences. When this was completed we took the geese to get them dressed, that means cleaned. There was a place down the road that does it for $3.00. First they cut off the wings

and feet. Then they have a machine that removes
all the feathers. It is a large drum with some
wires coming out that turns and you set the
goose on it and it pulls out the feathers. Then
they dip the goose in hot wax and pull off the
wax and this removes all the remaining feathers.
Next they cut off the head and gut the goose.
Once this is completed they just generally clean
it up and put it into a plastic bag.

From there we drove back home without any
problems. We left about 2:30 pm and arrived at
home about 7:00 pm. We were very tired but also
very excited, especially me because this was my
first goose.

NOVEMBER 7

I missed class last Wednesday because of the flu
so last night was the first time we met in a week.
Whenever I have missed a class, for whatever reason,
I return with the nagging fear that none of the
students will be there. Maybe they'll figure out
that they have very nice lives even without an
English class two nights a week. To my relief, just
about everyone showed up. I did get a few phone
calls in the late afternoon from students who were
checking that there would be class.

After thinking about and rereading the papers
that Richard and Gary and Paul had read last week, I
decided to read the class the piece I had written
about my float trip. The students laughed a bit,
asked me some questions such as ''Do you think
you'll go on any more canoe floats?'' and Paul said
he, personally, was glad I hadn't drowned because it
would have messed up his semester to have to break
in a new teacher.

As I was about to begin the activity I had
planned for the evening, observing and writing about
a person, Carol said that she wanted to talk some
more about my essay and about the papers from last

week. ''Why is it,'' she asked, ''that we so easily accept the stereotyped sex roles we are handed?''

''What?'' I said somewhat preoccupied by the fact that I wanted to start what I had planned and have a ''good'' class on my first night back. Carol was not intimidated.

''You know,'' she continued, ''we all thought it was perfectly natural that the men who read last week had successful experiences in the outdoors and that you, a woman, nearly drowned when you tried to get by in the woods.''

Carol had really caught me off-guard. There I was so busy thinking about what I had planned that I wasn't paying attention to what was going on all around me. I don't even have to stop and think anymore to say ''he or she'' instead of ''he'', I am very aware of who is given the check in a restaurant when I am with a man, and my skin crawls when I hear the name of Phyllis Schlafley. I am, to put it simply, a knee-jerk feminist and not only had I failed to see the connection Carol had made, I had contributed to it. I had been perfectly willing to cast myself in the role of female klutz.

When I explained all this to the rest of the class, Paul interrupted to point out that while there had been big trouble on my float trip, there were men on the trip too, that I had finally saved myself, and that I was after all on a float trip and not at home watching soap operas. I chuckled to myself here because I really do watch the soaps whenever possible.

Carol agreed that Paul was probably right. But she went on to say that no matter how much we know better, we expect men to excel at physical things—hunting, fishing, outdoors activities—and we still shake our heads knowingly when a woman does not seem particularly able.

''This might be off the beam,'' Pat interrupted, ''but I've noticed that whenever Angela asks us to work in small groups in class and have one person take notes, one of the women in the group ends up being the secretary.''

I was beginning to think that I was witnessing the sexual revolution right in my classroom and nobody was talking about sex.

On and on they went, recounting stories from their jobs, their classes, their families, while I listened and doodled on my note paper nervously. It was clear that the class members were exchanging ideas and insights and that some of them were trying to fit their ideas in with what other people were saying, some not so successfully and some not at all but I was suffering from that nagging doubt, ''Is this what a comp class ought to be doing, doesn't this belong in a human relations or a sociology class?''

I'd love to be able to say that the discussion rounded out neatly and everyone came away with more open minds and richer understanding of what sexual stereotyping does to us. Maybe that did happen, but all I can say for sure is that class time ran out and so everyone left, anxious to avoid being locked in the building since they all knew the security guards often start chaining the doors well before the designated ten o'clock building lock-up.

And so here I sit, Tuesday morning, wondering why, even though I had ten years of ballet lessons as a girl, no one taught me how to run until I was thirty and why, even now, I have to fight my inclination to offer to take notes whenever I'm in a meeting that does not have an official secretary.

NOVEMBER 8

Here is a piece from Don Hensley's journal

    desperate deserted streets
    dark lonely hide away
    morning sun eclipses clouds
    thoughts chase one another about

like a rolling picture on the TV tube
voices, sounds, noises, VOICES!
white eyes glisten, sliceing the darkness
-something is watching me-
laughs echo off metalic doors
closing behind me
pools bubble, whirling underneath
''losing my grip''
uneasy in everyday life
choirs sound the triumphant chant
the meaning of LIFE unfolds-
spring flowers shoot the heavens!
quicksand molten moss ripples
leaving silloettes of the sprouted roses
only the stems hold firm
to the life they once knew
as babes in the wilderness
tomorrow came a long way
to cloak them in glory
they sparkle, shining as no other
while thousands bowed low
before their magentic beauty
the garden surrounding them
a setting of rich contoured hues
adorned upon gloss against their presence
wholly unto themselves -
they fought the fight
for colour
each exquisite beyond bounds
but before the sun's westward setting

a HUMAN HAND reaches for the shears-
''one sharp slice and we're on our way,
    we'll race home this handful of bouquet''

    -only the r o o t s were left,
    to hand down a legacy of glory
    from which their fore fathers began
    a new beginning in rich soil

Seeing Kevin's and Don's work sent me back to
''Every Woman'' which has been on my desk for awhile
waiting for me. Since I was bothered by the three
middle couplets I played around with them for
awhile. . .

>> I changed ''Who offers no secrets but his
>> flesh
>> And sees no mysteries but hers

>> to ''Who offers no secrets but flesh
>> And sees no mysteries

but that didn't seem to make any kind of sense, so I
rewrote it as

>> ''Who offers merely flesh
>> And asks for nothing more.

I'd been working with the pattern for each
couplet of starting the first line with ''who'' and
the second line with ''and.'' At this point, I'm not
sure whether that is just an exercise in form or
whether it really makes the poem be what it is. I'm
inclined to believe that the pattern will have to go
because I think that I'm writing things to fit the
pattern instead of writing things that really say
something.

>> I changed ''Who gives used gifts requiring
>> no display
>> And understands a bargain made of
>> silence''

>> to ''Who gives used gifts
>> And bargains in silence''

>> Then I tried ''Whose gifts are used
>> And bargains unspoken.''

So this is what I have now. And I must admit, I
am not happy with it.

110

Every Woman

Every woman should have a lover

Who arrives at 9:20
And leaves at 11:20

Whose tastes are simple
Once on top, once on the bottom

Whose gifts are used
And bargains unspoken

Who offers only flesh
And wants no more

Who puts down the toilet seat
And helps her make the bed

Who dresses quietly
And leaves while she combs her hair.

I'll look at this again tomorrow. I promise.

NOVEMBER 13

It's tomorrow.
I've been thinking about the couplet ''Whose gifts are used/ And bargains unspoken,'' and it struck me that either I don't know what I'm trying to say about gifts and bargains, or it isn't worth saying. At the moment, I inclined to believe it a combination of the two and the best thing I could do is throw it out altogether.
I suppose that while I'm feeling tough about cutting down the excess in this poem, I should also get rid of the couplet which follows that one, leaving me with this poem:

Every Woman

Every woman should have a lover

Who arrives at 9:20
And Leaves at 11:20

Whose tastes are simple
Once on top, once on the bottom

Who puts down the toilet seat
And helps her make the bed

Who dresses quietly
And leaves while she combs her hair.

   Now the jump from ''once on the bottom'' to
''Who puts down'' is too abrupt. But it's three
o'clock now, and if I don't get ready for school,
I'll miss my four o'clock class.

NOVEMBER 14

   I think I've got it the way I want it.

                    Every Woman

     Every woman should have a lover

     Who drops by once a week
     And stays two hours

     Whose tastes are simple
     Once on top, once on the bottom

     This lover should

     Put down the toilet seat
     And help her make the bed

     Dress quietly   .
     And leave while she combs her hair

Chapter XII

You're now probably starting to develop more of a feeling for your readers; that is, you're probably thinking about their needs—what they'll need to know in order to understand what you have to say—when you write. What has to happen now is that you have to establish this attitude as a habit. I remember when I was learning to use a handsaw: my dad told me to put pressure on the saw when I pushed it down and to let up a bit when I pulled the saw back. I knew exactly what to do; that is, I knew it in my head. The problem was that the rest of me didn't "know" what to do. My arm, hand, shoulder, and back hadn't got used to the notion yet. So I got the saw hung up in the wood a lot. After I had done it over and over and over and over, though, I had the habit—I never knew what my father's instructions *meant* until the knowledge was really a part of me, until I got the feel of it.

Now as a result of all this telling, discussing, writing, and reading you no doubt know that when you wrote those games or activities the first time—before going through all the talk—you could have included a lot of information that would have helped the reader to understand more completely.

This all means that you know—as I first knew about sawing—that one important trick in writing is to include all that information. But just like me when I learned to saw, you have to do it quite a few times to develop the sense, to get the feel of it. Here are some chances to practice.

 Write about yourself—some quality that you have, would like to have or wish you didn't have. Break into groups again and read what you have written. Again, every time you come to a spot where you want to add something, mark the place, but from now on go ahead and tell the extra information to the others. See how much you'd really like to add. And again rewrite afterward to get a feel for writing it. (Watch especially at the beginning: do you find that when you're reading you want to fill in the listeners with a little background information?)

My students many times find themselves adding stuff before they start reading; if you do too, that means you should write down the extra information. (Remember that what a listener needs to know, a reader certainly will need to know.)

Write about how it feels to ride a motorcycle or a fast car or a roller coaster. (One paper I got included the sentence "Then coming down like a rocket going up." That sentence said a lot to me, does it to you? If you have never been on a roller coaster, does the sentence make sense?) After you've finished the writing, break into groups again and do the group reading and rewriting thing.

Go to the supermarket on a Friday night or some time when it's busy. Just walk around until you see someone who interests you. Observe for a short bit—just to fix that person in your mind. When you leave the market, go through the following steps:

First, review in your mind what interested you about that particular person in the first place. Was it a matter of appearance? Or was it what the person was doing? Or was it how the person stood, or walked? Or was it something the person carried? Or all or some or none of these things?

Second, jot down the actions or whatever interested you—just enough to help you remember what was important to you. Note everything you don't want to forget about your subject.

Third, of course, is to write about this person who caught your eye. Write the piece over until you are totally confident that you are communicating. Then read your piece to the class.

Now that you've looked over at least the last three writings (the one about your personality, the one about the fast vehicle, and the one from the supermarket visit), think how they are similar in at least this one way—you have hooked a label on yourself, on riding, or on a person in the store ("easy to please," "frightening," "funny"). These labels are based on your understanding of the labels, which is based in turn on your own unique experience. In order to communicate how you or the motorcycle or the shopper fit these categories, you pass on to your (listening) audience those details which led you to the label in the first place.

If, for example, you claimed that you are selfish, you found it necessary to show yourself being selfish. You told a couple of stories which showed how you fit into that label, "selfish." And the stories you told were probably typical of the experiences that led you to your conclusion ("I am selfish") in the first place. Perhaps, too, you had to tell the reader exactly what you mean by "selfish." In explaining what you mean by the word, you again probably turned to your own experience—or you made up experiences—to explain yourself.

Back to the writings about you, the motorcycle, and the supermarket character. If, in the second piece, you wanted your readers to know that riding a motorcycle made you feel free, you had to define that experience for them, you had to tell them what you meant. Imagine: you get off your first ride on a cycle. Friends rush up to you demanding to know all about it. You answer "Free, I felt free." And then you drop the subject right there and walk away. They probably would have some idea of what you had felt, but the idea would be more related to what experiences they connect with the sound "free" than to the experience you had on the motorcycle.

You'll want probably to tell about the wind and its effect, also what happened to your mind when you saw the road whizzing by underneath you. also the sense of balance as the bike leaned from side to side. And you'll tell this without having to study or think or turn to a style book. You'll fill in these details because they will help clear up the bewildered look on their faces; any you'll fill in with these details because they're the ones that led you to label the trip "free."

When you wanted to tell the others about that ragged woman you saw at the supermarket, or about that amusing-but-sad old man at the lettuce counter, you found out you had to expose the bottom of the iceberg I was talking about.

NOVEMBER 16

This entry is from Kevin Friel's journal

do you know

how

degrading it is

to have to

pay

to have something

iri

kevin d. friel

Chapter XIII

When writers are trying to communicate, what they want more than anything else at that moment is to help their readers to understand. They are genuinely concerned with their readers, not with themselves, nor with how clever their ideas might be. They want the reader either to understand something, or to be able to do something. Sometimes they go so far as to want the reader to be happy; mainly, however, what they want is that their readers have something added to their heads—the writers' idea. It's an act of sharing.

Slight digression: It would be possible here to get sidetracked in matters of what words the reader can understand, or what words they'll listen to. For example, a writer has to choose words carefully when writing to children. They use certain words for their mothers, some others for friends, and still others for children. As a matter of fact, that notion leads, I believe, to self-conscious writing—or speaking—which just makes a nervous wreck out of the sender and sometimes even the receiver.

Ever notice how uncomfortable you are when someone is very, very carefully choosing his words? Or how about the man who talks to children as thought they hadn't grown past the crib stage? I'm sure you've had teachers who spoke as though you were barely alive. My idea is that if the writer wants the reader to understand, s/he should be able to write just the way it comes out, naturally.

Perhaps have a mental picture of the audience and then let the words come the way they come. Since I've mentioned children, and since an adult writing for kids is especially apt to play a false role and choose his or her words super-carefully, I'd like to show you some examples of writing that some children like very much. The writers not only cared that the listeners would understand, but also that they would enjoy the writing. The first one is by Jim Pearson:

> Once upon a time or two ago there was a charming little valley nestled between two mountains. One of the mountains was called West Mountain and the other Not West Mountain.
>
> In the valley beside the tall trees and fields of green grass, with patches of daffodils scattered about, ran a beautiful winding river with blue waters that reflected the cotton like clouds that drifted by overhead. Everyone in the charming little valley called it the Beautiful-winding-river-with-blue-waters-that-reflects-the-cotton-like-clouds-that-drift-by-overhead.

Now, if you were to climb to the top of West or Not West Mountains, whichever one you liked best, you would see three quaint little villages. They were named Baden, Laden and Taden. It was a good thing too, because that's what everyone in the charming little valley called them.

In Baden they made the best bacon in all the valley. In fact, they make the only bacon in the valley. In Laden and on the farms close by the lettuce and tomatoes were the finest in the valley. Of course, no one else raised lettuce and tomatoes. The smell of fresh bread from Taden drifted all over the charming little valley. That's right, it was the very best because the only bakery in the valley was in Taden. I bet you knew I was going to say that didn't you.

In Baden the favorite food was bacon. They ate bacon three times a day and when they went on picnics they took bacon. The villagers of Laden didn't eat all of that bacon because they were always full of lettuce and tomatoes. How they loved lettuce and tomatoes! Now, everyone knows that in Taden they ate bread. They ate white bread, rye bread, wheat bread, and on Sundays they ate toast. The birds and animals ate the berries and greens that grew all over the valley and the river with blue waters that reflected the cotton like clouds that drifted by overhead provided plenty of food for the fish. Everyone was happy.

Now, if we look away from the three little villages and look across the farms and the woods, do you not see what I don't see. I don't see any fish swimming in the beautiful winding river with blue waters that reflect the cotton like clouds that drifted by overhead. When we look overhead there are no birds flying in the blue sky with its cotton like clouds that drift by and reflect in the beautiful winding river with blue waters. And no matter how hard or long we look we won't see any little rabbits and fluffy tails hopping along the banks of the beautiful winding river with, let's just call it the little river, O. K.?

In years past there were birds, rabbits, deer and all kinds of furry and cuddly little things scurrying and fluttering about. Now, not a creature was around. They all left long ago. As many fingers and toes that you have ago, plus two ears and a nose ago. You see, oh so long ago all the creatures lived happily in the charming little valley. The fish could be seen jumping and swimming about and turtles too would poke their heads in and out. The singing of birds could be heard over the little animals running about beneath the trees. A curious deer could be seen peeking into a low hanging birdsnest in a cottonwood tree. Everything was just as you and I would like it to be. The people of the three villages would picnic in the country and children played all over the charming little valley. That's its name you know, but hardly anyone calls it that anymore.

Now, I guess you're wondering why all the fish and animals left the charming little valley that laid between West and Not West Mountains.

It began one afternoon when the mayor of Baden was overheard to say "Our bacon is so good it should be the only food in the valley." When the mayor of Laden heard this he said, "Why that's absurd." (This is a word that grown-ups use when they mean "silly.") "Everyone," said Laden's Mayor, "would be much healthier and happier if they ate our lettuce and tomatoes." "Bread, Bread!" cried the mayor of Taden. "Bread, that should be the only food eaten in the valley!"

Things wouldn't have been so bad if the villagers could have stayed in their villages and kept to themselves, but the only candles made in the valley were made in Baden, and the other villagers had to travel to Baden if they wanted to light their homes. The only oil for heat on chilly mornings and to cook with came from Laden, and the salt to cure the Baden bacon and to put on the tomatoes of Laden and the matches to light the oil came from Taden. Because this is the way it was, the people of the three villages had to travel from village to village every day.

At first the people of the different villages just ignored each other as they passed one another in the valley. The villagers wouldn't let their children play with those of the other two villages. The women wouldn't speak as they passed those of the other villages. The men wouldn't speak to outsiders (those are people that don't live in their village).

Then one day as a villager of Baden passed a Tadener, he was heard to mutter "Bacon." "Bread!" yelled the Tadener. "No, lettuce and tomatoes" shouted a villager of Laden. The fight that followed was just the first.

Finally the fighting and yelling got so bad that the birds and animals stayed away from the villages, but as the feud spread over the valley, the animals left one by one until none remained. The birds flew over the mountains of West and Not West and the fish swam out of the valley not to return. The other animals went into Not West Mountain to live because that's where the little river began as a little spring that didn't have a name because no one but the animals had ever found it.

If you were to get up real early one morning you would see the sun just beginning to peek over the top of Not West Mountain. Down in the sleepy valley the three little villages of Baden, Laden and Taden would be just beginning to stir. You would see the sunlight as it dances across the little river and play tag with the dew drops on the green grass. Oh, if only there was the chirp of a bird, the glimpse of a ripple of water caused by a fish swimming by, or the sound of little feet scurrying across the fields. But don't look for it because it's not to be. No, not this day, we're to be without the beauty that comes with our friends in the woods.

The villagers are up and about and the feud is on as it has been for ever so long. Do you remember how long ago it was? Think back and you'll recall it was as many fingers and toes you have ago, plus two ears and a nose ago.

One day as a butcher from Baden was passing a farmer from Taden on Forest Park Glen Road, it happened. As they approached each other, a tomato fell from the farmers wagon. Stopping his wagon the farmer got off and picked up the tomato. Thinking that the farmer was going to throw it at him, the butcher let go with a slab of bacon that missed the farmer and hit the baker who was following close by. The baker was very angry and quickly grabbed a loaf of bread and threw it at the butcher just as a misguided tomato landed on his head.

There they were, the three of them throwing and shouting and throwing some more. The people from all three of the villages, upon hearing the racket, rushed to see what was happening. Now, when the villagers arrived upon the scene, they saw the butcher, baker and farmer covered with bits of bacon, tomato, lettuce and bread. What kind of bread? Do you remember, there was white, rye and—that's right—wheat. Seeing such a funny sight someone started to laugh. We all know that laughs are like yawns, when one yawns, it spreads to someone else and on and on it goes. So it was with the first laugh. It caught on and passed from one to the other until everyone was laughing as hard as they could. The more they laughed, the funnier the combatants looked. (That's another grown-up word for a fighting butcher, farmer and baker.) When they heard all this laughter, they stopped fighting and looked around to see what was so funny.

One by one by one, that's the three of them, they realized that they were the cause of all the laughter and they started laughing too. Now, everyone knows that you can't be mad at someone when you're laughing.

The laughter was heard all over the valley and you could hear it all the way to the top of West and Not West Mountains. All the birds heard it, all the animals that once lived in the valley heard it . . . and I bet you've already guessed that all the fish heard it. If you guessed that all the fish heard it, smile . . . I thought so. It sounded like such happy laughter that they all came down to the valley to see what was going on. They were curious because it has been so long, long ago since anything like this was heard. How long ago was it? Think back . . . You remember don't you? Let's say it together. It was as many fingers and toes that you have ago, plus two ears and a nose ago.

Now, what do you think the birds, animals and fish saw when they reached the valley. There they were, all the people from Baden, Laden and Taden having a picnic along the beautiful winding river with blue waters that reflected the cotton like clouds that drifted by overhead.

Those from Baden were eating Bacon. Those from Laden were eating Lettuce and Tomatoes, and guess what those from Taden were eating. That's right, Bread. "What's this?" said one of the grown-ups. "What's that lad over there eating?" "Why has he got everything put together?"

"Say that looks good!" said someone else.

"Let me have a bite," said another.

"Let's all make one!" shouted someone else. And they did. They really did. They all put bacon from Baden, lettuce and tomato from Laden and bread from, let's say it together, Taden, together. And that day they made the very first Bacon Lettuce and Tomato sandwich.

"What shall we call it?" said one.

"A Baddenwich," said a man from Baden.

"No!" shouted a lady from Laden. "It's plain to see it should be called a Ladenwich."

"A Tadenwich sounds much better," cried the mayor of Taden.

Before a new fight could start, a small voice said, "A Baden, Laden, Taden would be nice." So that's what it became known as.

The valley became quite a peaceful place once more and everyone lived happily ever after, except it seemed like such a waste of time to ask for a Baden, Laden and Taden combination sandwich everytime you wanted one, so after a time it became known simply as a BLT.

When grown-ups go into a restaurant and ask for a BLT, they think it means a Bacon, Lettuce and Tomato sandwich, but you and I know better, don't we. It's really a Baden, Laden and Taden, isn't it.

The afternoon Jim read that to my kids and me, I could see by the looks on their faces that they really liked it. But more than that I could see that he really was sharing an idea with them; he was deeply involved with them at that moment—the exact attitude that I believe any writer has to have when setting words down to communicate. So I thought, "Hey, that's an idea for a class activity: have the students write a story for some little kid. It might work." I tried it a few weeks later and it did work—the students got a much deeper understanding of what caring for the audience means, and they enjoyed the activity.

Here's how I gave the activity: I suggested to my classes that after choosing a brother, niece, son, or friend, they write something the kid would enjoy. After writing the story they were to read it to the child and watch to see what happened. If any parts needed clearing up, they could rewrite it if they wanted to. Then they were to come back to class and read their finished stories for the rest of us.

Barbara Holmes has a nephew named John—he's three and the one subject in the world that interests him more than anything else is the singer James Brown; Barbara said John was really pleased when he heard this story:

Guess who came over to my house last night? James Brown!! He was driving a brown and black 225 just like your daddy's car or should I say your car. He was wearing bell-bottom pants like yours and a Glen Campbell belt. No, John, Glen Campbell was not with him. When he stepped out of the front seat, two men from out of the back seat jumped out and said, "James Brown for Falstaff." James Brown threw off his red cape and shouted, "I feel good," And started to do the James Brown dance just like you showed me after you had seen him at the Kiel. Yes, John, I told him you lived in the 1300 block of Union. He said he would have come over but he knew you would be sleeping. But he did tell me to tell you to "take it slow" and "be mellow."

That's just nice, easy, natural writing—and it worked.

Another of the writers in class, James Barron, has a fat little nephew. Here's the piece Barron wrote for Robert:

Once a boy named Bobbie lived close to a great desert. But he had a farm and because he was not in the desert his farm had all the water and good land needed for growing good foods. His livestock was the best in that part of his country.

But he did not eat just enough food to make him feel good—he would eat so much until sometimes it would make him sick. Then one day he looked in a mirror and saw a fellow that looked in a mirror and saw a fellow that looked somewhat like himself. But he was so fat that he could not believe it was himself he was looking at. Still he did not stop over-eating. And so he continued to gain weight.

Then that day came when he could no longer get out of his house because he could not get out of the front or back door. That meant that he could no longer take care of his farm.

So he began to get hungry when the food supplies in the house ran out. He sat around and laid around his house, because he couldn't walk for long because of his great size. He became weak and his stomach hurt all the time. This is called starvation.

While this was taking place his farm was having its trouble. It had begun to rain and the water had begun to flood.

Mr. Robert lost all his livestock and the food he had growing on his farm. And the rain kept coming down until his very house moved. But not far.

When at last the rains stopped he found that he had lost so much weight that he could walk better, even run. But he was still weak.

The reason I wanted you to know this story about fat Mr. Robert was to show that bad conditions do not always come from outside ourselves, but sometimes from within!!!

I'm particularly fond of that story myself. For one thing, there's Barron's concern for his nephew. I have a feeling that Robert and Mr. Robert both like food more than is perhaps good for them. But also there are nice touches that only come when one human being is sharing something with another, like "This is called starvation." No attempt to talk down to the boy, just a simple matter of one human explaining whatever he thinks is necessary for another human being to understand. Also the notion of sticking on a moral has a certain charm for me—it's like Barron cared for the boy too much to just entertain him; he also wanted him to be better off. Plus the moral says to me that Barron figured any kind of worthwhile story should have a moral, so he made sure that his story had one—and not just any old moral about eating too much; that wouldn't be good enough for fat little Robert. Nothing but the best would do—a moral about good and evil at the very least.

Now, of course, it's your turn; you try it:

Think of your sister or nephew or even a little kid down the street. Decide what that one particular human being is most interested in. Then write about it. Care about the kid; think only about his or her understanding and liking whatever you're writing.

When you're finished with it, try it out on the person you had in mind—read it to him or her. See what the effect is; did they like it? Did they laugh where you intended something to be funny? Were they scared where you wanted them to be? When the story was over, what did that one important human being do? But most important: Was there any place in the story where the kid didn't seem to understand? Rewrite it until you're satisfied everything is cleared up—add whatever you felt you had to add when you read it to your friend.

Then, take the story you wrote for your friend and read it to the rest of the class—or if the class is too large for everybody to read his, break into groups and take turns reading them to each other.

One important thing to notice with each of these pieces is that the major factor for each writer was the choice of subject, not the choice of vocabulary— that just came naturally for a couple of reasons. First, you had that one person in mind and you probably couldn't use words that wouldn't be understood. Second, and more importantly, when you chose your subject, you chose something that the audience would like; it was then necessarily something the audience would understand. The subject, to a large degree, limits the vocabulary: if you're talking about cooking, "boil," "broil," "mix, "salt," and "beaters" would likely occur sooner or later. If you were talking about baseball, they probably wouldn't. If your subject was sledding, you wouldn't have any need to use the terminology found in nuclear physics. So when you chose your friend's favorite subject, chances are that the vocabulary wasn't "above their head." (I use quotation marks because I think there is a lot less than we think that is "above" kids' heads.)

Professional writers depend on choice of subject for their success: they find subjects which interest people and then write about these subjects—I mean newspaper writers, as well as novelists and the like. But for most of the rest of us, choosing subjects is not a calculated thing, not something we talk about for hours and think about for days. It's just that if we want to communicate, we have to care for the reader, sometimes even to the extent that we tailor a subject for the reader.

It's only when we're trying to *change* people that we choose subjects foolishly: when we *care* for our reader and when we really want to *share* with them we'll automatically choose more wisely: that's something we learn when we're very young. Remember when I said that I like pigs: Well, my kids know how much I like pigs, so the following paper came naturally to my eight-year-old daughter when she wanted to write something that I would like to read.

PIG

PIG WAS A PIG WITH PINK EARS. PIG WAS VERY HAPPY PLAYING IN THE MUD. ONE DAY PIG FOUND A LADY PIG WHEN HE WAS IN THE MUD POOL. PIG SAID OINK OINK! THE LADY PIG SAID OINK OINK! TOO. THEY GOT MARRIED AND THEY HAD TWO BABY BOY PIGLETS AND TWO BABY GIRL PIGLETS. . THE FOUR PIGLETS GREW TO BE BIG PIGS. AND ALL GOT MARRIED. . AND HAD THEIR OWN PIGLETS. AND THEIR PIGLETS HAD PIGLETS OF THEIR OWN TOO. AND IT WENT ON LIKE THAT FOREVER.

BY   LISA FRIEDRICH

124

See what I mean by things not being above their heads? Whitman devoted a lot of poetry to that same thought—generation producing generation producing generation. Well, here's little Lisa Marie. She said to herself, "I think I'll write something for Dad." Automatically, because she was concerned with me at the moment she wrote about pigs. That's the kind of sensitivity and attitude a writer has to have or recapture before becoming a writer.

NOVEMBER 17

The children's stories brought to class last night were so delightful that I am just going to include them here without comment.

The making of things by God
by Joice Coffman

There is a place that's far far away above the skies, and its name is heaven. The person that live there is very wise and strong. His name is God. He made everything living; you and me, all the bugs, birds and animals, the flowers and grass. God was a very busy man. Since he was so busy making things, he picked out some people to help him with his work,

St. Peter, St. Michael, St. John, St. Luke and St. Matthews, he didn't want to get them mixed up and call somebody the wrong name, so he called them all angels.

The angels job was to decorate and dress all the animals God made.

They had hair, feathers, paint, combs and
brushes all over the floor of heaven. They
worked hard, because God said they would do all
the work in six days, and then they could rest
the next day, and dress up for church and sing
in the choir.

They dressed the lion in hair and painted it
yellow, and sent him roaring down the ladder
from heaven to earth. They painted the giraffe
yellow and put some brown spot on him and sent
him down the ladder to earth. He almost fell on
the ladder, because his long neck got hung. Then
they put a ballet suit on the ostrich, a dinner
jacket on the penguin, and stuck some more
feathers in the peacock's tail to make it look
like a fan, and they left heaven for earth. Now
they decided to put some more hair on the
yorkshire terrier dog to make him look pretty.
They used the rest of the paint on the snakes,
to try to cover their scaley skin. They put the
last of the feathers on the turkey, and he went
gabble, gabble down the ladder to earth. The
angels thought they were finish, when they
looked and God had made a pig. There was no more
decoration left, so they let the pig go down the
ladder to earth without decoration. They said,
''he doesn't know any better.''
Soon as the pig reached earth, all the other
animal started laughing and making fun of him,

because the pig had no decoration. The penguin said ''Hey look! He's naked.'' Then the giraffe said, ''he has no paint.'' The lion roared, ''he has no hair.'' The turkey gabbled ''he hasn't any feathers'' and they laughed and laughed. The pig sat down in a corner and began to cry.

Now, owls are very wise, so the old owl said to the pig ''stop the crying; you go back up that ladder to heaven and complain.'' The pig started drying its eyes, and back up the ladder to heaven he went. The angels were gathered around, watching God make Adam & Eve when the pig arrived. The angels really didn't want to be bothered, but since they were angels, they are too kind to say no. ''What do you want?'' they ask the pig after it oinked several times.

Please angels, ''could you give me some little something to be proud of? All the other animals say I'm naked, and laughed at me. God heard the pig and  ask the angels ''why wasn't he dressed.''! ''Dear God, we used all the decoration up on the other animals and had nothing left, except what we saved for Adam & Eve.'' God said to one of the angels, ''Give me those curling irons''. The angels handed over the curling irons and cautioned ''God they're hot''! ''Ah!'' said God just the thing. He took the pigs straight little tail and put a big pretty curl in it. The pig looked over its shoulder, saw the curl, squealed for joy, and trotted back down the ladder to earth very happy. That is how the pig got their curly tails and no one laughs at the pig any more.

A EASTER STORY JUST FOR YOU
<u>QUENTIN</u>
by Brenda Conner

Momma Joya

Daddy Joya

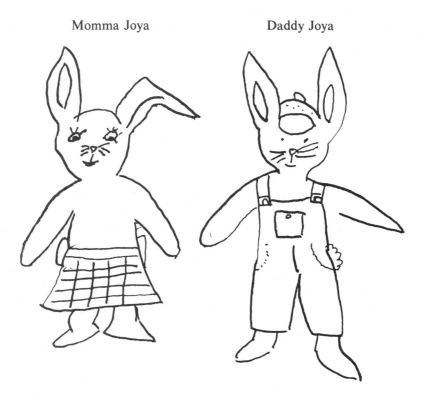

P.J. Joya

Sarah Joya

Quentin Joya

Once upon a time there was a rabbit family named the Joyas. The Joyas were a happy family. They really enjoyed one another. There was Daddy Joya, Moma Joya and the three smaller Joya's. The three smaller Joya's were named Quentin Joya, Sarah Joya and P.J. Joya.

One day the smaller Joya's were out playing in the fields near their house. They loved to play in the fields. Because there were all kinds of greenery to play in even to eat because they loved greens. While they were hopping and playing and hiding from one another they heard laughter. This laughter was not like their own. This brought them to a standstill. They all had puzzled looks on their faces.

Then Quentin Joya said to Sarah and P.J. lets hop a little closer so we can take a look. P.J. turned to Sarah and asked who is that Sarah? Sarah said I don't know in her softest voice because she didn't want them to hear her. Then she turned to Quentin and asked him who it was? Quentin then whispered in his somewhat deep voice its human kids. Then Quentin gave them a wave with his hand to come a little closer. So they hopped a little closer but not too close because they didn't want to be seen.

The human kids seem to be very happy and excited. P.J. began to count them 1, 2, 3, 4, 5, humans he said. Then Sarah put her finger to her mouth saying s-h-h-h. Then Sarah asked whispering why are they so happy? Then as they watched they saw something in the big humans hand he was going to read something. He first read in a deep voice The Easter Bunnies. Then the smaller kids began to clap their hands and smiles swept their faces.

As the big human read on he was reading about colored eggs and about the easter bunnies that would bring them. This seemed to make the children very happy. As the small bunnies stood quietly a flash of sadness swept their faces. Because they didn't have any colored eggs for

the children. They had never even heard of
colored eggs. So Sarah whispered lets go home,
Moma Joya and Daddy Joya would know all about
the easter bunny and his colored eggs. They know
everything. So they turned and hopped away as
quietly as they could.

When they got home they all rushed in the
door at the same time trying to talk at the same
time. They were so excited that Moma Joya who
was preparing salad stopped what she was doing
and rushed to the front of the house. Daddy Joya
who was relaxing in his favorite chair reading
jumped up and was right behind her. When they
saw the expression of the children faces they
didn't know what was going on. Daddy Joya said
hold on one at a time. So P.J. began to talk he
told Daddy Joya about how the story about the
easter bunny and the colored eggs made the human
kids so happy. And how worried they were because
they didn't have any colored eggs to keep the
human kids happy.

So Daddy Joya said in his high pitched voice
come little ones let me tell you the story all
about easter. Because now you are big enough to
deliver colored eggs on easter morning. So Daddy
Joya told the small bunnies how when it was time
for them to deliver eggs the bunny fairy would
come with all his magic colors. Then we will all
go down to the end of the fields with our wheel
barrels and collect eggs from the hen house.

Then he told them how Moma Joya would cook
them all in a huge pot of water. After the eggs
were cooked the bunny fairy would give them all
kinds of magic colors. The colors would be the
job for the small bunnies they'll get their
paint brushes and be as creative as they could
be. Then we will set the eggs out to dry. Then
just before day light you'll load them all in
the wheel barrel and take them to the humans
doors.

Then we will hide in the tall grass to see
how happy the little humans would be to get the
colored eggs.

Chapter XIV

One idea I've been stressing over and over again is that when we use words we should be interested mainly in communication. And that being interested in communication means that the receiver is the important part of a communication situation.

Isn't it amazing even to have to mention that—much less discuss it? Like killing is bad, or causing suffering to others is evil—concepts that everybody agrees with, but few act on. At any rate in class one night we got pretty far out in the discussion—as we do often—and a girl named Marion came up with the idea that the act of communication is an act of love.

"Well," I said, "that might be a bit strong. I mean, it's important and even beautiful to see people communicate. In fact, really communicating and knowing that communication is happening is one of life's happiest—but love?"

"Yeah, love. Look—love involves two people wanting to share, right? Let's say I've got a warm feeling inside, you know?" (Roars from the rest of the class but Marion was really concentrating on getting me to understand.) "So I want my boyfriend to have it too. Well, that's what communication is. Me wanting another person to have what I've got—happy news, a good joke, interesting facts—whatever. When I have a place to swim on a hot day, I want somebody I love to feel his body move from hot stuffy air to cool water too."

I was getting a bit warm myself, wishing that Marion would get off the examples she was using.

"And when I love somebody, I respect them the way they are, right? Same thing with communication—you talk to the listener the way they are, not the way you think they should be or something. You're not out to change them; you're too busy trying to understand what they have to know so they'll follow what you're saying."

I hadn't expected Marion to be so persistent about her idea, and I really wanted the class to get on to some other material, but I was watching her struggling with an idea she was developing in detail as she talked. Besides, it seemed likely that I was about to learn something.

"And just like love—if you want to do a job of it, you got to open yourself up; you've got to trust the other person enough, so you can take a chance that they won't hurt you when you open yourself."

I was starting to catch on to what she was saying. "Yeah and that's dangerous, isn't it?"

"No. Risky, maybe, but—well, at least I don't see 'dangerous' as the word. Like 'risky' doesn't seem so strong to me."

"O.K., risky."

That really was a better way of putting it, I guess. If you tell somebody what's really inside you, you're taking a risk. I'd never even thought of communication and love as being similar kinds of activities before: and certainly I'd never thought of communication being a form of love. But I was beginning to see it.

The thought was rattling around when class got out.

I got back to the office and turned on Angela's tape recorder to listen to what she had taped for me the previous night.

Out in the hall these two guys were yelling at each other, and because I was having a hard time listening and I was in a playful mood, I taped their argument. Besides they were wildly angry and I wanted to hear what heated them so. I think what Marion had said about love and communication must have been working in my brain and somehow this argument connected with it. No matter—I was lucky because the argument firmed up the love-communication connection for me. Here's what I heard and taped that day.

A: What?

B: Legalize marijuana.

A: Legalize marijuana?

B: Yeah.

A: Legalize marijuana! Man, you must be kidding.

B: No, marijuana should be legalized.

A: It should not.

B: Why not? It's as safe as alcohol and that's sure legal.

A: No it isn't completely legal.

B: Huh? What're you talking about?

A: Well, I'll grant that it's partly legal, but you're not completely right when you say it's legal—it's not for people under twenty-one.

B: Oh come on, you know what I meant. Nobody can buy pot without being subject to arrest. O.K.? That clear to you, stupid?

A: Sure. It's just that I can't accept what you say when it's not true, you know. I got to know to take the words you say for what you think. It's like communications, man. You got to get across to me what you mean.

B: Oh. You knew what I meant. You're just . . . well that's not the point. We were talking about legalizing weed, not about communication and jive like that.

A: O.K. Now what you were saying about that?

B: I don't remember now. What were you saying?

A: Don't ask me. You're the one who had the pot about to be legal and the whole country turning on and then getting hooked and dying of overdoses.

B: Overdoses of pot? Man you must be crazy.

A: Now who's being picky—I didn't mean pot. I meant overdoses of the hard stuff—and you knew it. Didn't you?

B: (Can't help himself—he begins to laugh): Yeah. O.K. I'll tell you what. You promise not to pull that bullshit and so will I. O.K.?

A: O.K.

B: Now where were we?

A: Let's see.

B: Oh. I know—

A: I had simply pointed out that using weaker drugs like marijuana leads to using harder drugs. That's where we were, right?

B: Right. And that's about the silliest thing I ever did hear. Harder drugs, shit! Man, I smoke marijuana and . . .

A: Yeah and look at you. Ha! Ha! Ha!

B: O.K. smartass, you gonna listen or joke around?

A: Well, it was just a little teasing. I'm sorry—but god—you didn't have to—

B: Oh come on. I was just joking too. You are dumbest goddam . . .

A: What do you mean dumb?

B: Well, you don't even catch on that I catch on and then you don't even catch on that you don't catch on that you don't catch on that I catch on. Just dumb enough to think that pot leads to bad drugs.

A: You smoked pot?

B: Yeah and I've never dropped a pill or shot junk in my arm.

A: Yeah but can you prove that you won't? You don't know that.

B: Yeah but can you prove that I will?

A: Sure everybody knows that it leads to addictive drugs. Everybody does.

B: How can you make a generalization like that?

A: Like that? Like what?

B: Like you just said—"Everybody knows that marijuana leads to drugs."

A: Well, don't they?

B: I don't.

A: Yeah, but you're just an exception.

B: Well, what makes you think that marijuana does that?

A: You can't say what you're going to do, or what you're not. You can't prove to me that you'll go on just with pot.

B: And you can't prove to me that it's harmful. Facts prove that about 5 percent go on to harder drugs.

A: That's not what I heard. I heard that—

B: And anyway what're you talking about—hard drugs?

A: Hard drugs, you know—

B: Yeah, like martinis or something.

A: And where are you getting your facts from?

B: They're just the facts—like America was discovered in 1492 or the earth is round—stuff you don't have to prove—stuff everybody who's been alive and paying attention to the stuff he sees knows. Man, I don't know what you've been doing, but those are the facts.

A: No they aren't.

B: Yes they are.

A: Well, I don't believe them.

B: Do you think, are you saying I'm a liar?

A: No. It's just. . .

B: Yeah, right.

A: Well, what kind of hard stuff are you talking about?

B: Like LSD.

A: LSD? Man, LSD is another scene altogether.

B: No it's not, yeah, man, that's where you go from pot.

A: Weed is like taking a couple of sleeping pills.

B: That's what you say, not what I say.

A: That's all it's like.

B: You prove it to me.

A: You prove that it's not. . .

They went on like that for a long time. But I stopped hearing them and turned off the tape recorder. I kept thinking about what Marion had said about love and sharing and communication. When you're trying to communicate, you're trying to share. You have an idea or a feeling and you want somebody else to have it too. Yeah. O.K., Marion—what're you gonna do with those two guys? Surely they're trying to communicate—all you have to do is look at them to see that they're in earnest. But they're damned sure not trying to share anything at all. At least not anything like happy stuff. Calling each other dumb and crazy and stupid. They're far from bringing anything but pain to each other.

It reminds me of that old telephone tease: "What're you doing?" "Talking to you, stupid." The answerer rejects the attempt of the asker to set up a communication system by intentionally denying the real meaning of the question (something like "I called with no particular purpose in mind, but would you be interested in talking anyway?") Instead, the answerer insists on taking the words for what they literally "mean."

The two guys arguing about marijuana did the same thing: right at the start when they got on what "legal" means, and shortly after when A got mixed up about "overdoses" of marijuana.

They're standing there talking; they each want the other to understand; they each want the other to change his mind (for whose own good?) so they're certainly interested in the listener.

Let's stop right here and look back over the argument.

What was communicated? B wants marijuana legalized—that's what he sends to A—and in return A sends the message that he disagrees. And little else. Paltry sharing if you ask me—and of course without sharing much there really isn't communication. And it's pretty sure they're not in much of a loving, sharing situation. And so I came to understand what Marion had come to. Let me share with you the rest of my thoughts on the subject. Not to convince you, but rather to share my way of seeing the problem with you so you can come to your own understanding.

Actually what we're talking about is one of the oldest and most respected of communication forms: argument or persuasion. I think that's what "rhetoric" was originally about—techniques and forms to convince people. Of course, through most of our school lives and even nonschool lives we are led to believe not only that it's possible to convince others of our own positions (THE TRUTH) but also that it's our duty to carry this TRUTH to others less fortunate than we are. After all, if I'm lucky enough to know the TRUTH, and if others know it not, I'd be selfish not to bring others around to my way of thinking.

And of course there are techniques to accomplish this.

Earlier I said, "Writing is not a matter of skill, it's a matter of attitude." At least that's the way I see it. I doubt there are techniques a person can learn to bring others around to TRUTH. That's the conclusion Marion and her classmates came to when we discussed how arguments work.

We listened to the tape of A and B several times. The same notion—that they were in no sense trying to share anything, that actually they were in no sense trying to share anything, that actually they were trying to hurt each other—kept coming up. As one student pointed out, "They're trying to beat each other; communication is a matter of helping." It was clear to all by the end of the hour that this argument, at least, was neither love nor communication.

 You might like to look over the argument carefully and discuss at what points in the conversation you see a difference between trying to communicate and trying to hurt or beat. Try to get inside the two arguers and check out what you think their attitudes are.

Judy Edwards brought me an argument that she had written. I'm really fond of it for several reasons, so I'm including it here. Notice, while you're reading it, that it's like a written daydream. You know—when you've just had an argument and you keep it going in your head an hour after you and your opponent have finished? At any rate, Judy's argument:

The characters are B.J. and Mr. R. The scene is an interview.

MR. R: You were chosen by what we call a random sample. A certain amount of people are selected to represent a particular group, and you were "luckily" selected from this area to represent the young people of your age group. Have you ever heard of the "Kinsey Report?" I am sure you have. This is the same, so to speak, set up. However, I will not ask you personal questions about your sexual life. That is up to you . . . (*With a nasty snicker Mr. R continues*). Well, ah, at any rate, you may refuse to participate with the project; however, we, or I, would like you to stay.

B.J.: (*In a disgusted tone.*)Yeah, sure. I guess I'm here and you're there, so I might as well stay. It may be interesting after all. I can refuse to answer if I wish?

MR. R: Yes. Of course.

B.J.: Good. I'm ready!

MR. R: Fine. The first question is "How old are you?"

B.J.: It is improper to ask a lady her age. How about if I say between 20 and 25?

MR. R: Sure. Secondly, were you raised in the country, such as farm, rural, so forth; or were you raised in the city?

B.J.: I was born on a farm, lived on the farm, worked on the farm, educated on the farm, and foolishly left the farm when I was 16 years old to live in the big city.

MR. R: Well, fine. Okay, now, what race are you?

B.J.: Pardon me, sir?

MR. R: Ah. . . . what race are you, Negro, Oriental, or white?

B.J.: "Race" is a wild word, sir. You could use it in so many different ways. Do I really have to answer that question?

MR. R: Well, I guess we could overlook it; however, it would help if I knew whether you were white, black, red, etc.

B.J.: Well, sir, my race is . . . ah . . . *human!* Yes, my race is the human race.

MR. R: What! I mean, pardon me!

B.J.: I said my race is H U M A N. Does that answer the question you asked?

MR. R: NO! NO! (*Said in bewilderment*)I mean are you black, white, etc., or what!

B.J.: Does it really make a difference?

MR. R: Oh, of course not. It is just one of the questions.

B.J.: They should change the form and omit that question completely. Can we not forget about skin color and just be open minded?

MR. R: It makes it difficult for me.

B.J.: Why?

MR. R: Well . . . it *is* just that I would like to know whose opinion I am recording. It is nice to know who to credit with the opinions.

B.J.: I have an idea. Just write in "human" at the bottom.

MR. R: I cannot do that. Are you white or black?

B.J.: What are you, sir? Can you really answer that question for me?

MR. R: Of course I can, but I am the one who is asking the questions.

B.J.: Yes you are, but I don't believe you know what color you are.

MR. R: Of course I do. I'm white!

B.J.: See. I told you. I don't believe you are really white. What do you think of when you say "white?"

MR. R: Well . . . white is a color without a color. It is not black, red, brown, or any of those.

B.J.: I hate to shatter all the beliefs you have, sir, but you're also what you term as "colored." Surprised?? Have . . .

MR. R: Huh! (*mumbling*) Young blood, young ideas, young beliefs.

B.J.: Yes. As I was saying., have you looked at yourself in a mirror lately?

MR. R: Yes, of course. Every day.

B.J.: What did you see?

MR. R: Myself of course. My own image reflecting . . .

B.J.: Did you see the pinkish or maybe reddish color in your skin? Maybe you're pale but you would still have color. You're not a pure white body. Have you ever thought about it?

MR. R: NO! I have not!!!! I am going to assume from this point on that you are white. Now . . .

B.J.: WHAT DO YOU MEAN—WHITE!!!! How in the HELL can you assume that I am "white." I am not white at all. You really don't listen, do you!

MR. R: O.K! O.K! I will not assume that you are white. I will assume that you are bl . . .

B.J.: No, sir, I'm not black either. I'm just a plain ole girl you picked at random to participate in this damn interview to represent my age group. Why do I have to be any certain color?

MR. R: Everyone is a particular color.

B.J.: No, they are not! Do you have a pet?

MR. R: Yes, a dog; and I would like very much to see him right now.

B.J.: What color is your dog, any particular color? Or is it just a dog to you?

MR. R: Well, my dog is silver and blackish-grey.

B.J.: Do its fur and skin colors make a difference to you? It sure is funny that we, as the superior beings, go through a process of elimination by our own private rules. Funny, isn't it?

MR. R: Well, young lady, I can see we are about to get into our own realm of ideas and I am not allowed to argue or influence any of the clients. We would be here the rest of the day if we were to continue. The rest of the interview is far too long to continue through with you, trying to get straight answers. So . . . well, good luck to you and I hope your bubbles aren't broken.

B.J.: *Bubbles* . . . ah, well, okay, sir. If that's the way you feel, but I don't believe that it was a complete waste of time. Before I leave I'd like to ask the purpose of the interview.

MR. R: It is a research project set up all over the nation to find out how the different races respond to one another.

B.J.: Oh! How do you feel about the different races?

MR. R: Ah, well, that is immaterial. Good luck in school, maybe the next time we meet we will be able to communicate . . .HA! But I doubt it.

B.J.: Yes, well, good-bye and have a happy, fulfilled life. May I add one word of wisdom before I leave?

MR. R: Sure.

B.J.: Well, sir, just don't stop too quickly, you may find your thoughts catching up with your spirit and body. God, how miserable that would be. Good luck with your future interviews. Good-bye, sir. (*Walking out the door*) I feel a great deal of compassion for you.

(*Slam!*)

I was really interested in her paper for a lot of different reasons. First of all she had to get her ideas straight enough to write them down, but she didn't have to organize them into a complicated essay. Second, she really enjoyed writing it and seemed pleased with it when she reread it in my office.

Also, while she was reading it, I kept recognizing it—but not the argument, or the situation of interviewing. No, what I recognized was the idea of a daydream argument. It's like listening to a discussion on the radio while driving to school all of a sudden I stop hearing the radio and begin to form my own little program in my head. I'll be listening to the mayor saying that the city needs an increase in the sales tax. "That way the people from the suburbs who have more money will contribute their share to the protection of the city," he'll say. Gradually, the radio program disappears and it's me and the mayor. "No," say I. "The poor people spend most of their income on goods—for which you'll have them pay a sales tax. The rich folks, who you say will pay their share, spend the horse's share of their income on services. Let's put a tax on tailor-made suits and on storing of furs and on gardening and landscaping services. Let's tax chartered helicopters and things that rich people buy." "Oh, no." retorts the mayor. "Anybody can afford a small tax like 4 percent and everybody should pay a little tax." "Oh, come now, your honor. If a family spends $20 per week on groceries because that's all they have, your 'little' 4 percent means a loaf of bread they can't buy, or a quart of milk." And on. And on.

One of my students told me last week about a daydream argument she often has. Her mother is a nut on having boys' hair short. The mother is always after Joan to have Billy's (Joan's son) hair cut. And Joan occasionally will find herself arguing with her mother—but just in her imagination Joan says, "_____," and then her mother comes back with "_____." But Joan then answers with "_____." And on. And on.

In fact it seems like that kind of daydreaming—he'll say, then I'll say, and he'll come back with, but I'll answer—is something all of us do.

So back to Judy. She wrote an argument from her imagination—something which demanded that she had her mind straight. And she liked doing it. So, the next chance I got, I introduced the idea to one of my classes. And it worked.

 Just sit back for a bit and remember the last time you were inspired to have a daydream argument with somebody. (The President? your brother? your history instructor? your boyfriend or girl friend?)

(1) When it starts coming back, write it down just the way it comes to you. Or better yet—take some disagreement you are having right now with somebody. If none of these works, that is, if you can't seem to get into an argument with anybody, watch the news tonight or else one of those talk shows on TV or one of those radio shows where people call up and tell what they think about local issues. Soon you'll find yourself arguing with somebody. Write it all down.

(2) When you've finished writing, type two copies of your argument. Or else write two copies legibly. Type or write, just make sure you have two readable copies of your argument for the class.

(3) Next, break into groups of two. Give the other person one of your copies and take one of his or hers. Then act out the two arguments, one at a time. Only, don't read your own part. For instance, if you and I were partners, first we'd exchange papers—I'd give you one copy of mine and you'd give me one copy of yours. Then we'd flip a coin to see whose argument we'd do first.

Let loose, really act it out. Try to feel like the character you're portraying. Don't worry about making too much noise.

(4) Read each other's parts.

(5) After you've finished, have the whole class discuss the experience. Talk about how you felt. Did anyone do such a good job of getting into your opponent's part that you began to sympathize with him or her? Discuss this switch if it happened. How did you feel toward the person who was reading your part of the argument? How did you feel having to read the lines which you wrote for the opponent in the argument? When you were reading your partner's argument, how did you feel about him or her?

Here is another complicated activity. Do it step by step.

(1) Divide the class into two groups and assign each group one side of an issue regardless of their actual belief.

(2) Get together with your group and write a position paper, showing why your group's attitude is the right one.

(3) After each group has completed its position paper, read them to each other, after choosing one reader from each group.

(4) Then return to your group and prepare rebuttals.

(5) Read the individual rebuttals—first one pro, then one con—until all the individual rebuttals have been read. Take notes while your opponents are reading.

(6) Discuss as a class: Who won? What does "win" mean in an argument? Is the winning side the side which has the best arguments? Or is it the one which convinces the other side? Or is it the side which is "right"? Which were the "best" arguments? What constitutes a "good" argument? Cleverness? Truth? What's clever? Or true? According to whom?

(7) Discuss: What were your feelings during the debate? How did you feel toward the opponents? How did you feel when "they" came up with a "good" argument? Did they come up with any? What do "they" think about that? How did you feel when someone

on your side came up with a "good" argument? How did you feel when you came up with a "good" argument?

(8) Get off by yourself and review this whole activity. Contemplate especially the attitude and the emotions you had during the debate. Compare your attitude toward the other side with the attitude which Marion and I claim is necessary to communicate.

NOVEMBER 20

Class ended about an hour and a half ago. I met Dick after I left school. We ate salads and talked about how this journal is progressing but mostly, I fretted about the class that had just concluded. Dick kept telling me to relax, that I'd know what I needed to know Wednesday night. Finally, he said, ''Hey look, you're just spoiling your dinner and you're spoiling mine. Just go home and talk to your dog.''

Well, I did go home, but my dog is asleep so here I am talking to myself, or my typewriter, or whoever it is who is reading this journal.

I am upset by what happened in class this evening; and Dick's right, I'll know Wednesday whether I really had any reason to be worried so I should just wait and see. But I'm going to try to write about the situation and maybe that way I will have a better grasp myself of what went on. And if that works, I'll be better able to analyze what the students have to say the next time we meet.

(If I haven't mentioned it before, I've learned over the years that writing about something can be a very valuable way of figuring out what it is you think or feel about it. Granted, this kind of writing may not always be the most polished or successful but it can be quite useful. Writing doesn't always spring from a complete, prior understanding. Journal writing, in particular, is often a conversation with yourself in which you figure something out.)

For class tonight, I had asked the students to think of a number of currently controversial topics from which we would select one for class use. As soon as class started, we were in trouble. I asked people to name the topics they had come up with so I could write them on the board. Then we would be able to select one for the whole group. I was putting the topics on the board and fielding the usual good-humored complaints about my handwriting. The list on the board was growing: the ERA, abortion, reinstituting the draft, busing, public housing, legalization of marijuana, nuclear energy, capital punishment.

''There's no way I'm gonna talk about that Equal Rights Amendment. It's stupid and that's that.'' Walt Jamison had spoken and I was astonished. I didn't remember that he had been particularly vocal when we had talked about sex stereotyping and other related issues and I began to wonder whether he'd been fired or had a fight with his wife before coming to class.

''This is just a list from which we'll pick a topic, Walt,'' I said, ''if you don't want to talk about the ERA then you probably won't have to.''

Clare, who was sitting next to Walt, got a very earnest look on her face and in a somewhat shaky voice said, ''I think that we shouldn't throw a topic out just because one person doesn't like it. Maybe that just means that it's a good topic since he got all worked up about it.'' Clare is a fairly serious, thoughtful woman so I squelched my instinct to joke away some of the tension. Instead, I figured that I could defuse it by changing the way in which I was handling the activity.

''I tell you what,'' I said, ''why don't you get into groups of about four people each, and we'll have each group come up with a topic.'' That way, I hoped that the disagreements would be on a smaller scale.

''I don't think that fair,'' said Clare. ''You're just trying to avoid the issue.''

Every once in a while, I regret that fact that I prefer a somewhat unstructured, informal classroom. And tonight was one of those times. I felt that I had to answer Clare, but I also didn't want to hit whatever nerve in Walt that had sent him off in the beginning.

''Okay,'' I said, returning to my desk. As usual I was sitting in a student desk toward one side of the room near the door. I always say that it's so I can get out first if anything awful happens, but the students and I both know that is is because I am more comfortable teaching in a less rigidly divided atmosphere than the one provided by a teacher in the front of the room with desks lined up in front of him or her. Also, I believe that a slightly disorderly looking classroom is unsettling to the students and much more conducive to learning. The students should know me and each other, but things needn't be exactly the same every evening, or we all get lulled into oblivion. All this is by way of saying that my authority in the class, my position as leader, director, whatever, was being questioned and so I had to avoid an impulse to sit down at the teacher's desk in the official front of the room. It would have been a nice sanctuary but a cheap way out. One little gesture, sitting in a desk I never use, and I would have told them all that I, after all, was the teacher, so I was the boss.

''Let me tell you what I was planning to do this evening and then you can decide whether we should go on.'' At that point I was hoping someone would suggest that we all go home and watch Monday Night Football.

''Dick, you know, the guy with the beard and the office across the hall? Well, he told me about an activity that he had used in his class and so I thought I'd try it. The idea behind the whole thing is to try and understand how arguments work and to figure out what kind of communication argument is. But we weren't supposed to get an argument started so fast. It was supposed to go like this: first, pick a controversial topic; second, divide the class arbitrarily in half, without regard to which side of the issue individuals prefer; third, have one group take one position and the other group the opposite position; fourth, have each group prepare a statement supporting its position and select a spokesperson to address the other group. After all this is done, the two groups sit facing each other on opposite sides of the room and the spokespersons present their cases. After this, the groups re-convene and prepare rebuttals and then we go through another round of presentations. Okay?

Walt was looking a bit chagrined by the time I finished my explanation.

''Sorry everybody got so stirred up,'' he said, ''but we're studying the history of the women's movement in my American History class right now and I just got assigned that topic for a debate in my oral communications class and I'm fed up with the same old thing.''

I acknowledged his explanation but it still seemed that his reaction had been rather strong.

''I think we should do ERA,'' said Clare. ''Walt probably knows a lot about it now and anyway, I think it's really important.''

I wasn't sure quite what that meant but Willy and Pat and Loretta and Gary were all agreeing and no one seemed to be objecting any more so I said ''Sure.''

''We've already used about twenty-five minutes of class time,'' I said wearily, ''so let's get going. Everybody north of Pat is in the pro-ERA group and everybody else is against ERA. Take about fifteen minutes to get your opening statements ready and then we'll start.''

I then left the room as fast as I could and went over to my office across the hall to see if I had any coffee left in my thermos. Even though I probably shouldn't drink coffee during class because it gets me even more worked up, there is something very soothing about holding a hot mug and smelling good coffee.

There was a half cup waiting for me and I found
a piece of fudge wrapped in plastic in one of my
desk drawers so I treated my frustrations with oral
gratification. It was a feeble remedy, but I didn't
care.

From across the hall, the sounds of rising
voices reached me, but I didn't budge. Fifteen
minutes was what I had said and I planned to stick
to it.

As I walked back into the room, I could hear
people from both sides of the room announce to their
opponents that they had really good arguments and
somebody was going to lose this one.

The groups quickly lined up opposite each other.
Both groups put their spokesperson in the middle of
the line. It struck me that perhaps I _was_ watching
Monday Night Football. Clare was speaking for the
pro-ERA group and Loretta was speaking against. I
thought it interesting that women had been picked by
both groups.

Clare went first. And what happened as she read
was very revealing. Wouldn't you think that the
group with the floor would be sitting there smugly,
pleased to have the first say, confident that by
voicing their opinions they were gaining ground. Not
so, Clare's group were all slouched back in their
seats with their arms folded, except for two who
were doodling nervously, and, almost on cue, took
turns glancing furtively at the other side. And
there, on the other side of the room, sat these very
self-assured people listening attentively, upright
in their desks or leaning forward, listening. All
but three were taking notes. I wondered what was
going on. Clare's group had put together some good
arguments in favor of ERA and she was reading
clearly. Why aren't they happier. Shouldn't they be
feeling good about their presentation?

My puzzlement continued when Loretta began the
argument for the other side. Clare's group was
transformed into alert, attentive listeners; and
Loretta's group seemed to abandon her physically as
they began to slide down in their desks and drop

their heads. I was beginning to think that the class had gotten together while I was out of the room and planned this little ballet as an entertainment for me. Then I remembered that Dick had told me to pay attention when the presentations were being made, that I might be surprised. I was wondering if this was what he had been warning me about.

During this first part of the activity, I acted as a moderator telling each person when to speak and reminding any interruptors that they'd get to speak later. Dick had told me to do it that way and suggested that I might want to abandon the moderator role during the rebuttal phase and become just an observer. He was right.

After the initial presentations were finished, the groups retired to their corners and prepared their rebuttals. It only took a few minutes so we were ready to continue at 9:30, leaving twenty minutes before the end of the period.

The groups lined up again, and once again, Clare read first. But before she had read two sentences, Paul, who was on the other side, interrupted her to say that their rebuttal wasn't fair.

''Why don't you wait till she's finished,'' defended Carol from Clare's side of the room.

Clare continued, only to be interrupted once again, this time by Loretta who asked where the ''pros'' had gotten their information. Willy answered for the ''pros'' by pointing out that Walt was on their side and he, as everyone knew, was studying the women's movement. Clare, trying to get things into a more orderly groove, suggested that the other side hold its questions till she had finished. Loretta said that she thought that was a good idea. So on Clare went with her rebuttal.

By this time I must admit, I wasn't really listening to her reading anymore but was focusing all my attention on watching the people in both groups. As soon as Loretta had spoken for her group, Paul and Pat began whispering to each other and making notes. Every member of Loretta's group had turned to someone else in the group and they were all talking to each other. The only person still listening to Clare was Loretta herself who must have felt some responsibility to remain silent since she had made the promise.

Finally Paul interrupted Clare again and told her that her facts just weren't straight and that her group had misrepresented what Loretta's group had said in their original statement.

Clare lost her temper and told Paul that if he and the rest of his group had been listening he wouldn't have said that because he'd have known better and she knew he didn't support women's rights and that was stupid and arrogant and what could you expect from a man anyway.

That was it; Clare was yelling at Paul who had two weeks earlier written in his journal about why he thought ERA was probably a good thing even though he hadn't always thought so. Loretta was looking frustrated. Walt who had thought the subject silly in the first place was defending a man's right not to have greater demands placed on him because of his sex. Carol was trying to get the members of her group to calm down and Gary, who had always been mild, in a quizical sort of way, was claiming vigorously that women needed to be protected from all sorts of threats.

I couldn't keep track anymore but I do know that the culmination of the melee came for me when Sarah, a small fragile-looking woman of about thirty looked across the room and announced quite loudly, ''you people are so damn sure of yourself don't you ever stop to think about what you're talking about before you open your mouths.'' This was Sarah who wrote in her journal regularly about how difficult it was for a woman alone with children to take care of them, find a good job and go to school. Sarah, who knew that her ex-husband didn't pay child support. Sarah, who was the class's informal authority on women's rights. Sarah was saying that the ERA was a bad idea.

Dick had been right. Strange things had happened. All the members of the class were involved in a free-for-all argument in which no one was listening to anyone else and a number of people were speaking passionately in favor of things they did not believe.

But time ran out. And they went home. Heading down the halls in little groups according to their side in the argument. I knew that would change by the time they got outside because Sarah and Carol usually take the bus together. And Willy drives Loretta home when her husband has to work late and keeps the car. But I was really shaken.

I didn't have time to talk to the class about what had happened and so here it is, quarter to two. I've been at this for over two hours and the only thing left on TV is the last fifteen minutes of Mannix. I think I know a little more about the dynamics of what went on tonight but I have to wait until Wednesday to find out if any of the class members will have thought about it.

NOVEMBER 21

After re-reading what I wrote Monday night, thinking about the class some more, and talking it over with Dick, I'm feeling a lot less apprehensive about the class tonight. Some of the problem was simply the natural interaction of the class members but much of it was just what Dick told me later almost invariably happens when he does this activity in class. People really do lose sight of what they are trying to do: they forget that their goal is to communicate some ideas on a particular subject and become so wrapped up in saying something and making points in the argument that they do not even notice whether anyone is listening to them.

Once the moderator is gone from the structure, you have all the makings of a brawl where the only real concern is making the point that ''I am right and you are wrong.''

Dick agrees with me that it is unfortunate that
we ran out of time before I could get the students
to step back and examine what had developed out of a
discussion of an issue that had not sparked much
controversy earlier.

NOVEMBER 22

A few people made jokes about Monday night's
class as I was checking off the attendance last
night, but no one seemed to bare any scars from the
confrontation. Loretta wasn't in class but she
called me in the afternoon to tell me that she had
hurt her hand at work and was going to stay home and
nurse her wounds. When she asked what we would be
doing in class I explained that we were going to
talk about Monday's class and try to decide how
argument had gotten in the way of communication, and
if, in fact, that was what had happened. She said
that she was disappointed to be missing the class
since she'd been thinking about Monday's session. I
suggested she write down her thoughts in her journal
so she could remember them for next week. She
laughed, ''It's my writing hand I hurt.''
Actually, I was probably more upset than any of
the students about the brouhaha on Monday, but I
suppose that's my job. Carol said that she had been
very surprised at how angry everyone had gotten but
that it reminded her of a fight she had had with her
husband over the weekend. They had decided to go to
a movie even though they were both tired after a day
of working on their house. She didn't care what they
went to see and he didn't either, but they ended up
in a fight, each accusing the other of picking out a
stupid movie.
I tried to explain to the class the theory that
communication is a form of love because it involves
a genuine desire to share and an interest in the
other person's response. ''If that's the case,''

chuckled Gary, ''we didn't have much love around here on Monday.''

Sarah said that she realized after class that she had been yelling at Willy in particular even though the two of them had had several conversations about equal rights for women and she knew they agreed. ''I really felt dumb, yelling at someone I like and agree with in support of something I don't believe in . . .''

We analyzed the argument for the whole class period, considering what we meant by communication, questioning whether argument was or could be communication, deciding what a person did communicate in an argument, wondering whether debate and argument are the same thing. Periodically, someone would interrupt someone else abruptly to make a point and then the rest of the class would laugh and make jokes about people who would rather talk than love or score points than score. All in all it was a good-natured and thoughtful class.

Chapter XV

Now I'd like to share with you what conclusions I've come to concerning "persuasion" or "argument." They're pretty much spun around what Marion had said: communication depends on the communicator's *attitude* toward the reader; that attitude has at least three elements.

(1) The communicator wants to *share* thoughts. A way of sharing is to decide what the other person has to know in order to understand the thought and put that information into words for the reader.

On the other hand, when I'm arguing, much of my attention is devoted to trying not to share; indeed sometimes I'm even trying to hurt the other person, to embarrass, to beat him or her. Probably you can recall this feeling. Remember being put down sometime in the past, then hours later thinking of a good retort—a good shot that would have really got to the other person?

(2) When I want to communicate, I must *respect* the other for whatever she or he is—a separate human being just like me.

But when I'm persuading, I have the obvious attitude that I'm somehow superior—I'm right and s/he's wrong and it's my job to straighten him or her out. I'm their salvation (whether they like it or not, whether they appreciate it or not—they need me), and it is my duty as a holder of TRUTH to manipulate those poor disadvantaged people to help them so that they'll be right too.

The flaw in this attitude is not only that it's incredibly arrogant to assume such superiority—but also that the other person is put into a position where they have to defend themselves. They are bound up in fending off their attacks and defending their own ideas from your judgment. No wonder they have little attention left to understand with. Surely you've felt yourself pushed into a corner and know how little you cared to understand. You can see how this sort of relationship is not very likely to produce communication.

Yesterday I really fell into this kind of trap. I urged in a faculty meeting that our group object to the check-out sheet procedure. At the end of each semester, all the faculty members are supposed to have the audio-visual chief sign a sheet saying we have returned all a-v equipment we checked out; then the librarian has to swear that we've returned all our library books; then the registrar has to testify that we've turned in all our grades.

I insisted that this procedure was insulting, that it implied we are thieves, and I said that we shouldn't put up with it. Some of the other teachers disagreed. I strongly implied that anybody who disagreed with me was a coward. The rest of the discussion consisted of people showing how they could accept the checkout sheet and still be brave folks. I had pushed them into a personal corner and never really communicated. Plus, of course, I had assumed that there was only one decent way to look at the problem—MY WAY.

Ironically, the very drive to convince tends to defeat the attempt to convince. That is, when I try to convince you of something, I am trying to change you, to manipulate you, to bring you from your present unimaginable ignorance into the bright sunlight of my own wisdom and truth. But you'll tend to defend yourself from this charge—and thus be less apt to be convinced.

(3) The third element in communication might be the hardest one to achieve—it's *trust*. When I decide to share an idea with you, I have to trust you not to hurt me or make fun of me or judge me stupid or silly or wrong. Or else I have to trust myself enough so that your judgment of me won't matter, because my ideas are a part of me and when I decide to share them, I open them—and therefore me—to criticism. Thus I have to trust both you and me; I have to forget about the judgments and criticism of me and simply try to share.

But, of course, when I'm in an argument, my attitude is the opposite of a trusting one. In fact, I'm probably deeply worried that you might have better arguments than I do, maybe even be a lot concerned that I might be wrong and you might be right. Perhaps that's why I try so hard to make you lose; that would show us both how right I am.

So I concentrate on not saying anything which you could refute too easily. In fact, what usually happens to me is that I try to say as little as possible— I just try to be more clever, more loud, more quick than the other person. I get sarcastic, emotional; I preach, and I pose as a really smart guy. In short, I try not to communicate; I try to win.

And you don't even have to be in an argument to feel this way. I saw something on TV last week that is an excellent example of this. A doctor connected with Ralph Nader was arguing with a power company executive about the effects of radiation. The audience was about evenly divided in their sympathies, about half with the doctor and half with the opponent. When the doctor would score—win a point in the argument—her half of the audience would applaud. Notice how you almost have to use the language of games— enemies, opponents, scores, beat, win, and so on? It is very much like a hockey game with an audience cheering and the combatants trying to attack and defend almost simultaneously.

And you could see them listening to each other—but not to understand. They were watching for an opening, a mistake on the other person's part that would lead to another score. Remember your attitude when you were listening to your opponents in the debate? And when you were preparing your rebuttal? Of course nobody trusted anybody, and nobody got communicated to.

Simply stated, I'd say competition kills communication. Argument leads—almost inevitably—to a competitive attitude. And an adversary situation—enemies fighting one another—makes genuine communication impossible, because it makes trust—trust of one's own ideas and trust of the other—too risky.

So what do you do about convincing? I'm running the risk now of trying to convince you that trying to convince is futile. I struggle with that by trying to keep my *attitude* straight—I'm really not trying to convince; all I'm up to is explaining my thoughts on the subject. Take them or leave them, all or in part—it's up to you. My ideas are just what I've come to at this point in my life. And I'm not particularly worried about being wrong—had plenty of practice in that.

Back to the question then: what do I do about convincing? Nothing. I explain myself as best I can; I try to communicate my idea. I work at trying to share, not hurt; trying to respect, not manipulate or change; trying to trust, not beat. It's all a matter of attitude, and sometimes I make it; sometimes I don't.

One notion that would probably be almost universally accepted is that impersonalization caused by machines is deplorable. Anyone who would want to argue that point would start off at a great disadvantage for sure. But what if he merely explained what impersonalization had meant to him and showed how it had made his world more bearable one day? No attack, no defense, just explanation.

Here is one such piece that David Kuester wrote some years ago:

IN DEFENSE OF THE IMPERSONAL

Today it's very fashionable to go around attacking the impersonalization that is occurring in our society. According to this line, the IBM machines are reducing us to robots, and we are irreversibly in the hands of the machines (like the ABM and MIRV) that control our lives. We no longer control them; they control us.

Or so the argument goes.

What I wanted to write about today was what happened to me today, or, to be more specific, some of the things that happened to me today.

I don't simply want to list them, and I couldn't tell them all for that would take too much time, so all I want to do is select some of them and select them in such a way that I have some idea running through what I write, not just a collection of details from my life—after all, things have a way of happening in a random way—but a collection of details sifted out by a human mind to make a point.

And that point—the lesson for today—is how wonderful the process of being impersonalized can be.

That's not what I started out to say, and that's not even what I was planning to say while things were beginning to go on in my life today, but, looking back on it, I'm sure now that that's what I want to say and I'm going to say it: the impersonal can be wonderful and more humanizing than the personal.

Let me explain.

This morning I got up at the crack of 10:30. Then I went out to lunch. Then came the errands.

For me, the routine—teaching and earning a living—isn't the challenging part of my life. That's the errands. The little diddlyshit things that I don't really have to do but should do and that, when you get right down to it, take up most of everybody's life. The errands.

I made a list last night.

1. License
2. Package
3. Bank

That meant that I intended to accomplish three things that day. First, I intended to get a new license plate for my car (the old one expired three months ago). Second, I was going to mail a package. Third, I wanted to get some money out of the bank (I'm always taking it out— seldom, it seems, putting it in).

So, after lunch, I left school, and drove home to get the certificate of inspection and personal property tax receipt. In Missouri, you have to have those two documents before you can get a license, and that's exactly why I was three months late getting mine. It's not a simple matter of going down to the license store and plopping down your money, and saying "Give me a license." It's more difficult. Much more difficult.

First, you have to get your car inspected. Then, when you find out that your car cannot pass inspection, you have to get your car fixed. Then, $231 later, after you've done all the things they told you to do to get your car in shape, you go back to the inspection station, and, since it's been thirty days, you prepare to wait in line again while they run your entire car through the entire process of state inspection again. You want to go out to lunch while they do this, but they tell you you've got to be right there for some reason, so you wait, and when they finish they tell you that your brakes need a new disk or new housing or new shoes or socks or something, and you write it down and promise them that you'll get it done if only they'll pass your car then so you can get your damn license, and you throw yourself, dramatically, at their mercy, pleading change of venue and talking in detail about the difference between law and justice, and hoping that the guy who sent your car through is a little humane and will understand and cheat a little on the form, and he does, and you've promised you'll get your brakes fixed, and you leave the inspection station, certificate finally clutched tightly in your hand.

Then there's the personal property tax receipt. You must have a receipt showing you've paid up all your personal property taxes. And though you have, indeed, paid all of your personal property taxes—after a good deal of haggling—they overcharged you the first time around—you can't find the goddam receipt and you call the office of the Tax Collector and tell him to send you a duplicate, and the clerk tells you they can't do that over the phone because you must send in a dollar, so you send in the dollar, and, sure enough, a few days later, a duplicate personal property tax receipt arrives, all stamped and official, and with that filed in your inside coat pocket next to the certificate of inspection you finally go over to the local license bureau to get the plates.

You walk up to the window marked "Fees" because what you're mainly conscious of is that this is going to cost you money—including a $5 per month penalty fee for lateness (you wonder about the constitutionality of this). The woman behind the sign marked "Fees" takes your hard-earned, argued about, and paid for receipt for personal property taxes and your certificate, bought at the price of making all sorts of rash promises to the man at the inspection station. She looks at them, puzzled. And then she looks at you with contempt and tells you you're at the wrong window. You must go FIRST to the window marked "License." So you go to the window marked "License" and hand her the hard-earned documents, and she looks at you coldly and says, "Where is your registration?"

"Do I need a registration?"

"I can't issue a permit without a registration."

"I don't have a registration."

"You don't have one?" She is genuinely shocked. She's worked at this job for years, and she's genuinely shocked—as though it's the first time a customer didn't have his registration. She keeps staring at me.

"Where do I get another registration?" I say.

"You can't," she says. "They only issue one."

I know I'm not the first person who doesn't keep his registration, and so I know there's a way around this, and, finally, I go over her head and talk to the supervisor who tells me that it is, indeed, true that I can't get another registration, but I can get a title if I write Jefferson City, and that's just as good, so I leave thinking I've failed to get the first thing on my list done, but that, in a way, I'm another step closer to the glorious day when I'll be driving legally again.

By now, it's pretty late in the afternoon, and I drive fast and angrily over to Famous Barr, the super department store of St. Louis, to mail a package. This is thing number two.

I park. I walk inside. I see a clerk.

"Where is the mailing counter?"

She stares at me.

"Packages?"

She asks the clerk standing next to her.

"It's on the first floor, next to notions."

I go to the first floor, find notions, and there's a window and I ask, "Is this for packages to be mailed?"

"Yes," she says, and, almost without looking up, she grabs the package.

"Just a minute," I say. "I want to write the address on one of those things."

"Things?"

"Address cards," I say, hoping that this is what she calls them. She seems quite official.

She hands me one of those things. I start filling it out.

"This package is already wrapped," she says her face all wrinkled.

"Yes," I say proudly. (That's another story.)

"What do you want me to do with it?" she says. She sounds critical now. She is obviously unhappy, and feeling superior, and is getting some kind of revenge for something. I don't know what.

I am tempted to tell her what to do with the package. "Just mail it," I say.

"Oh, no sir," she says. "No sir."

I'm sure it's a personal thing. "O.K.," I say. "What did I do wrong?"

"Wrong?"

"Why won't you mail . . . isn't this the counter for mailing packages?"

"No sir," she says. "Not this counter."

"You said it was." I tell her.

"I said it was the window for packages to be mailed," she says, contemptuously. "We wrap them at Famous Barr, but we don't mail them."

I pick up the package, and walk away. I'm too dejected to argue with her. I don't even care.

I look at my watch. It's after five o'clock, and it's too late to go to the post office, so it's strike two and I head for the bank. I drive fast. I pull in the old driveway for the old drive service. Quick and reliable.

But there are cars parked all over the place, in the slot where you're supposed to wait for your money, and all over the lot, and the back is dark and the lights aren't working, and they aren't signaling the cars through as usual, and it's like a ghost town. I drive up next to the old drive-up window—the one that used to have the blonde behind it—and there's a sign, "Closed and moved to 7707 Forsyth."

I don't believe it. The bank has moved!

So I drive to 7707—it's not too far away, and I follow the signs carefully, because it's all strange and modern and swoops of concrete and arrows, all rather free form and huge.

There are no people there to tell you where to turn, only explicit signs that direct you to various lanes depending on whether you want to deposit or withdraw or neither or both, and it's all very mathematical and laid out and impersonal, and I am delighted. Nobody to talk to. Hooray. I follow the correct lane.

And when I get to the booth, I look up and see a television screen— my own reflection in a TV screen. "Push for service." I push.

A voice comes out of the speaker, clear and in high fidelity. "What can I do for you?" It's the blonde! And as she speaks—miracle of miracles—her face appears on my TV screen. For me alone to view.

"Hi," I say.

"Hi," she says.

I look at her on my TV screen thinking it's strange to just see her image and not her, but her voice comes over loud and clear, and she looks good on TV, too, and we're both having fun with the new TV gadget, and she says "Hi" again, and a nice "How are you?" and I say "Fine" and how is she, and she's fine and I'm fine and everyone is fine.

"I just want to say I love everybody," I say.

She laughs and her image is on the screen and I can see her vibrate a little as she laughs.

"When did you move over here?" I say.

"Today," she says, still vibrating.

I reach into my wallet to get the check. It's from the insurance company—payment for an accident which caused damages that had to be fixed before I could pass the inspection to get my license—which, as you know, I didn't get.

"Just hand me the check," she says.

And I laugh.

"I mean put it in the cylinder," she says.

And I look and, sure enough, there's a cylinder and it's marked "cylinder" and I open it and there's a tube inside and I take the tube out and put it in my car next to me, and sign the check and get ready to put it into the cylinder. Only the tube is like a miniature vault. No matter what I do to it, it won't open.

"How do you open the cylinder?" I ask.

She comes back on TV and I have the feeling she's been waiting inside all the time for me to ask her a question before reappearing on TV, and, although she's stopped vibrating, she reappears and tells me to open the latch on the side. In a cold, impersonal voice. Not insulting. Just impersonal.

So I open the latch and sure enough the thing comes open, and I put my check into it, and put it back in the slot, and there's a whoosh like a vacuum cleaner, and suddenly it's her cylinder and I'm on TV.

"We can't cash insurance drafts," she says.

And, at that moment, I'm ready to leave without saying anything and go drive off a cliff somewhere or, at the least, have a couple of shots of bourbon.

"You'll have to deposit it and then withdraw it," she says. "I'll enclose a deposit slip."

And she does, and the whole thing goes whoosh, and then I'm on TV, noticing my profile and not really minding about the deposit slip, because I don't have to write Jefferson City or go back into another line. She's taking care of it all right here.

I am staring at myself for a moment on the monitor, and she comes back on and says, "It may sound like a lot of mickey mouse, but we have to put up with regulations." And she laughs at the absurdity of it all.

And I laugh at the absurdity of it all—I who sit in my little car not even reaching distance from the blonde with whom I am talking—I who have passed the whole day dealing with rigid clerks who don't know what they're doing and aren't doing anything anyway, and all of that is now forgotten, because, for the moment, on TV, she's my girl. Because she is so far away she can be close. Because she is so good at the regulations she can make fun of them. Because that TV is working so well we can admire each other at a distance, without seeming overly intimate. Because the whole thing is so click-click-click impersonal, we can be all the more real with one another when we're being personal.

And all the cliches about the impersonal disappear before my eyes— all the generalizations become suspect. For all the mickey-mouse little menial chores that my blonde used to perform—opening windows and closing them herself—don't have to be done anymore. She's free to talk with me. She's free to cash my checks better and be herself better, and the little mechanical things are all the smoother, and human error is being eliminated, which leaves humans free to have a sense of humor about that and about their own stupidities.

And I'm more comfortable.

And I've gotten something done.

And the blonde is smiling when I leave and tells me "Good-bye" and, as I leave, I think about cliches—words and expressions that have lost their meanings, have lost their power because we take them only at face value. We accept them only for what they are—words—and the meanings behind them are lost. And it occurs to me that the attacks on impersonalization are a cliche, too. They are an attack on machines for not being human. And they never take into account that machines can leave people to be human. They can free us from being menials. They can make it possible for us to share with one another—not arguments about where you send for a title for your car or where you mail a package—but ourselves. Our pleasing little jokes about how absurd it is to not be able to cash a check unless you deposit it first. Our smiles. The TV angles. And the important, basic, human need to rise above menial chores and use our minds.

No, machines don't make us into automatons.

That's up to us.

If it happens, we'll do it to ourselves, and we won't be able to blame them.

Maybe machines will take out our licenses for us—maybe they will send out duplicate personal property tax receipts by machine and send out duplicate titles by machines. Maybe then you'll just put all those into another machine and get your plates. Maybe machines will wrap your packages and mail them, too.

That will free us to do more things like writing, things that really do involve us as human beings.

You couldn't get more controversial than to defend the impersonal. Our defenses should have been up from the start; convincing us should have been nearly impossible. But we got convinced without even knowing it. Why? Well, one thing is that David didn't work hard to convince us about the way he feels; and he never said that everybody else should think the way he does. He simply shared his day and his mind with us.

David takes the position that impersonalizing can be liberating. I would ordinarily argue that the process is enslaving rather than liberating. But David doesn't argue, he explains himself: he shares with his reader those experiences which led him to his conclusion. He opens himself up so the reader gets inside him as he goes through his day: we can be confused and frustrated right along with him as he goes through the mess of getting a Missouri license. We feel half angry, half embarrassed, and half beaten when he tries to mail the package. And he allows us to share his relief when he chats with the girl at the bank.

We don't worry about attacking his logic, because he's not pushing us around. We don't feel inferior for having believed the Machine to be a Monster, because David's not attacking contradictions to his feelings. We're not threatened by being stupid if we disagree, because David's not competing with us or anyone else. He's just sharing his conclusion with us by sharing the experiences which led to that conclusion.

He's sharing himself—that shows us he trusts us. So we can trust him. He respects us—he doesn't even hint that we should change our minds. He's not attacking or defending; he's explaining.

What it boils down to is that he's not worried about convincing, he's trying to convince and trying to explain. And he ends up being very convincing. By communicating.

 You might like to go off by yourself for a bit and think about what significance all this has for your understanding of what human beings are: are we really all the same under the veneer of differences caused by differing experiences? Is what David touched commonness? Is that what communication is—touching a common source? What does that idea have to do with the idea I proposed earlier when I said, "Writing is more a matter of attitude than of skills"?

Another nonwriting activity. During the next couple of days, pick someone who usually doesn't agree with you about things (parent? brother? or sister?): forget about trying to convince him or her. Just try to explain. When you start feeling like you're back in combat—in an argument, when the emotions you felt in the debates and arguments start coming back, when you become aware that you're now trying to hurt the other person—STOP. TRY AGAIN. AND AGAIN. AND AGAIN.

One final writing activity. Go back to that argument-script you wrote before. Now write about the same subject you chose before. Has your attitude changed? If so, has that change in attitude affected what you write?

NOVEMBER 23

Kevin brought in some more writing yesterday.

strange faces
 aged
  younger than
smiles similar
though parents
  would have died
     of shock
watches are not
  worn at reunions
'tis a distant time
  refusing to be
different beginnings
   of sort
further lands
   seen
'n the voices
  of yesterday
 expressing a future
spacing the trees
 afraid of
    a closeness
doubting nature
  losing the clouds
what's wrong

how does failure

begin

the eyes tell

iri

kevin d. friel

Chapter XVI

Today is Monday. I'm sitting in the office here trying to write what comes next. Last Wednesday, Thursday, and Friday I was right here starting, typing, starting, sweating, swearing. Put in a new sheet of paper. Type. Get through two pages. Type. Read it over. Swear. Rip it out. Crunch it into a ball and throw it away. I kept wondering—how can I get this thing started? What kind of clever gimmick could I use to get the readers into it? Bell words, waves and icebergs, and all kinds of great notions have come to me before; why don't they now?

It's even affecting my private life. Thursday night when I picked up one of my kids, I acted the fool—the scene should be familiar to many. "What's the matter, Dad?" "Nothing." "Why the long face, then?" "I don't have a long face; that's just the way I look." Ursula, in the meantime, won't give up. "C'mon, something's bothering you." "Goddammit, nothing's wrong. Didn't you hear me say that two minutes ago? Nothing [very deliberately], nothing is wrong. Absogoddam-lutely nothing. Listen very carefully to the words I'm going to say. Try your very best to figure out what I'm intending to say. N-o-t-h-i-n-g i-s w-r-o-n-g." (Then back to driving down the street at about 60 mph.) Silence. Evil stares at any drivers who dare to drive alongside me. Loud horn for those who go as far as to place their cars in front of mine. "Dad?" "Yeah?" "What's for supper tonight?" "You gonna nag me about that now? I'm trying to write a book. I don't have time to go shopping and make up menus. What do you want for supper?" "I don't know. Something filling." "What's the matter with you? Just because I didn't have a six-course turkey dinner ready for you, you got to get mad at me." "I'm not mad," "Hell you aren't. Look at yourself in a mirror."

And on.

And on.

And on.

Yesterday was a quiet day and I sat down with me and thought some. Tried to figure out what was the matter with the writing that it was going so bad.

Lots of times I can't write because I really don't know what I'm talking about. I haven't thought it through enough, I don't have it all straight. I'm not, in short, really ready to write. But that is not the case this time. I know the material I'm going to write. In fact, much of it is written already—in my head. Why won't it go down on paper?

O.K. What's the problem?

And on.

And on.

Same questions. Still no interesting start. No gimmick to get the subject matter hooked on to. Then I think, "gimmick?—just say it; forget about being clever." But I don't. I keep remembering how I liked the last chapter. I can't let down. I can't write some old dull thing. I want to like it, and I want others to like it. I'm not thinking this stuff consciously yet—it's just notions floating around down there under my attitude and awareness right now.

Then I start remembering consciously how Larry looked when he told me how much he liked the last thing I wrote. Then I start remembering Angela's note—she told me she not only liked it but admired it. Then I finally think consciously—out there where I can see the thought. Could I be trying to do what I keep saying a writer shouldn't do? That is, am I writing to get praise? And not just that, but trying to get praise so much I'm forgetting that I'm writing to communicate to people? I'm trying to get praise from people I'm really not writing for, people who aren't even my audience.

Then the last desperate dodge—But what if this chapter doesn't come off like the last one did? What if it's not as good?—Come down, Friedrich. I see you now. I know what you're up to and it's stupid. Teacher—teach yourself. Write to communicate. Write so others can understand what you have in mind. Don't be worrying about how much you'll be liked. Be understood.

LET LOOSE. YOU'RE WRITING ABOUT THINGS YOU KNOW. JUST GET THEM DOWN. THEY'LL GO INTO PLACE AND MAYBE EVEN ANOTHER ICEBERG WILL HAPPEN AND MAKE THE THING WORK LIKE THE LAST ONE. WELL? DO IT.

So the lessons you might learn from this book are not ones we learn once and then know for good. No, they're like most things in life—a constant struggle. We forget from time to time; our attitudes shift every once in a while and we'll find ourselves back where we've been trying to move away from. We all have to relearn the same things over and over and over.

My experience trying to get this chapter going is what this chapter is going to be all about.

MESSAGE:

> IF YOU GOT SOMETHING TO WRITE,
> IF YOU KNOW WHAT IT IS,
> DON'T BE TRYING TO BUILD YOURSELF UP,
> DON'T BE TRYING TO IMPRESS PEOPLE,
> WRITE IT TO BE UNDERSTOOD
> AND LET THE ADMIRATION AND PRAISE COME OR NOT.

My notion is that a writer shouldn't worry about what others will think of him or her—s/he should worry about whether they will understand what s/he has said. The job is to make the statement with sufficient information in it so that the reader can understand it. Where I got stopped was in worrying about what others would think of me; it's really probably just as well that I didn't even start while all that was on my mind.

Let's go over this whole notion, but while we do that, let's keep in mind this one important idea. To a very large degree, writing is not a matter of skill. It's a matter of attitude, it's a matter of what's really in the back of your mind as you sit down to write.

I'll start with a picture of a communication situation.

The man on the left gets an idea—let's say he wants the woman on the right to pass the salt. So he produces signs—in this case mostly signs made up of sounds—which he hopes will carry his idea into the other fellow's head. The signs which he uses are, therefore, ones which he hopes will stand for the idea—not just in his own mind, but also in the mind of his receiver. These signs are called, collectively, the message. So there are three main elements which relate to the message: the idea, the sender, and the receiver.

I believe that how the message turns out depends on how the sender feels about the idea, the receiver, or himself, and on which one he feels is most important. For example, let's take the case of Julie and me eating dinner together. My situation is that the meat tastes flat and I want more salt on it, but Julie is sitting within arm's reach of the salt, so I want her to send it down to me. (That's the idea.) I (the sender) say, "Salt please." (That's the message.) Hopefully, Julie (she's, of course, the receiver) will not only hear the sounds I've made, but will translate them into an idea in her head—an idea which will at least roughly correspond with the idea I have in mind. And that's what understanding the message means.

Now, all this seems very obvious, and it is an easy idea to master. But we have to master it in our insides, not just our heads. When we don't, then we go through what I did starting this section.

Julie's understanding of the signs is the most important element in this particular case. In this situation I am concerned first with her. I'm willing to admit that what I finally want is to get the salt for myself, so that I will be

*I mean for the page to stand for whatever kind of signal the person uses—sound, gesture, writing.

165

pleased, and you could probably say that what is really important to me is me, not Julie. O.K. But during the signal sending, that is, while I'm talking, I've got to be first interested in her. Not in her health or intelligence or success in life—that's not what I mean. I've got to be interested mainly in her hearing a message which will translate into an idea like my idea.

When I wrote to communicate, what I am trying for is that the receiver's idea will look just like my idea; I am not concerned that the message look right. Of course, we do care about the message, but not as the ultimate goal. Many writers ask, as their *primary* concern, does this message look like my idea. That is, is this the right word for this idea? Or, when I read my message, is it like what I want to say? But what's important is not whether the message communicates to me, but whether the message communicates to my reader. That's what I mean when, in a situation where I'm really trying to communicate, I say the receiver is the one I care about.

 Here are a couple of activities for you to prove this notion to yourself. Sometime when you're talking to somebody about something really important to you (your future? your car? your boyfriend? your solution to one of your friend's problems?), watch yourself, or at least be conscious of yourself while you're talking. You'll notice that you watch the receiver very closely, maybe even squinting slightly; you'll watch for any tell-tale sign that s/he doesn't follow what you're saying. That's because they're your main concern for the moment.

Never forget the important part our listener plays in our communication. If you'd like to have some fun and also test out this importance, next time you find yourself in a conversation you're not particularly interested in, do some of the following.

(1) Show no emotion—vocally or facially—while the other person is talking to you; just stare blankly while s/he is talking.

(2) Keep looking bewildered while s/he's talking; pretend with your face that it's a language you don't understand.

(3) Laugh, look disappointed, pretend astonishment when what the speaker is saying calls for no such reaction. For example, if your friend is telling a joke, react as though they just announced the doubling of your income tax; if they're telling you a recipe, pretend they've just told you a joke to end all jokes; if they're telling about the party they went to last Saturday night, pretend they told you the solution to a complicated math problem and you can't quite follow; if it's about a new car or new clothes, act as though it's about the death of a pet dog.

(4) This one is for the phone. Don't say anything that shows approval or disapproval or interest or amusement. Just say "oh" whenever you feel the speaker wants you to say something.

One thing you now know for sure—you know how important the receiver is to the sender. A writer who succeeds translates this into an attitude. The main concern becomes the reader.

Think about it this way. Let's say somebody owes you $100. They're going to bring the money to your house, but don't know how to get there. So you write directions to get to your place. They might be the best spelled directions in the history of directions; the punctuation might be impeccable, the vocabulary spectacular. If they don't get there with the money, you're out. In fact, you might astonish them with the brilliance of your writing, they might be standing there on the wrong corner, mouth hanging open and scratching their head amazed at how well you write. But if they're also trying to figure out what you had to say, you lose.

When I say that 90 percent of all communication difficulties are related to a misunderstanding of the relationship of idea to sender to message to receiver, I think it's especially true of students and most especially true of students writing for class. In my experience most students are more concerned with how they sound than what they say—it *seems* that they are more concerned with the message than with the receiver; they want the message to be just so, but what they're really concerned with is themselves—with their own image, with what the reader is going to think of them, with how they are going to sound. Let's take a look at somebody trying to sound good.

> I would by no means wish a daughter of mine to be a progeny of learning; I don't think so much learning becomes a young woman. . . . I would have her instructed in geometry, that she might know something of the contagious countries;—but above all, Sir Anthony, she should be mistress of orthodoxy, that she might not misspell, and mispronounce words so shamefully as girls usually do; and likewise that she might *reprehend* the true meaning of what she is saying. This is what I would have a woman know;—and I don't think there is a superstitious article in it. (Sheridan, *The Rivals* I, ii)

The woman who's saying all this is named Mrs. Malaprop. She's a character in a play who has a word named after her. The word is malapropism, which means a "ridiculous mistake in word choice." For example, if you introduce an "extinguished" friend instead of "distinguished" friend, that's a malapropism.

167

Review what you know about how words are learned. We have an experience connected with a sound, "tree with ꝰ , and on and on. Until we have a general idea which connects and includes all those separate experiences. Then the word "means" something to us. Thus we develop a vocabulary—a list of words which "mean" something to us. When we talk to somebody, we choose words in hopes that the "meaning" we have is more or less similar to the "meaning" that the receiver has.

In that context, of course, it's impossible to use a word with a "wrong" meaning. The only way a person could use the "wrong" word would be if they intentionally said "tree" when the object they had in mind had never been connected to that sound before. If they say "yes" when they know the other person will understand the word as affirmative, but they know the honest thing to say would be "no," then I would say they're using the "wrong" word.

Look up the following words in the dictionary:

> "progeny" and "prodigy"
> "contagious" and "contiguous"
> "orthodoxy" and "orthography"
> "reprehend" and "comprehend"

Mrs. Malaprop says she doesn't want any daughter of hers to be a "progeny" of learning. We can guess that the word she "should" be using is "prodigy." In one sense I would argue that she is not making a "mistake." She is using the word which *she* connects with a very advanced child, one who knows a lot for her years. What has happened is that she has chosen a sound which will appear a "wrong" word to most of us; she has used a sound which will "mean" something else to most of us. But of course, in spite of choosing the "wrong" word, we think we know what she means.

Young writers sometimes think the only thing that matters is how they say things. Think about it first, then discuss how you feel when you write in your classes. Why do you really write? To communicate. Remember some of the things you've written for assignments in past years. Who were you trying to communicate to? What were you really trying to communicate? Were you more concerned with saying something? or with sounding good? Again it's a case of writers being most concerned with themselves, using words to build themselves up instead of to communicate.

Mrs. Malaprop is not a student (in fact she's not even a real person— she's a character from a play); however, I think we can learn from her plight. She claims that there is not a "superstitious" article in her speech. To me "superstitious" means giving people or things credit for having powers that they do not have. Like a rabbit's foot will bring good luck. When Mrs. Malaprop uses sounds to show off her learning, when she parades herself, when she slings words so that her receiver will think she is smart, she is giving words credit for having a power that they do not have—the power to make her wise.

Go back to the diagram:

Now for her the important thing is not what the message would ordinarily "mean," The message refers to a young woman's education; but the idea Mrs. Malaprop is really trying to communicate is "See how bright I am; see the impressive vocabulary I have."

Do you see a connection between her and your own attempt or my own at the start of this section? Most people laugh at her—she is meant to be a comic character. But when you think about her walking through life, constantly concerned that she will not live up to somebody else's standard, she is more a pitiful character.

Thus when I use words to impress rather than communicate, my main concern is not with the receiver or with the message. It is with me. Yes, I want the message just so; yes, I've worried about the receiver—but I'm worried over what the message will say about me; I'm not concerned with the receiver understanding, but with what the receiver will think about me.

And it certainly isn't just poor Mrs. Malaprop and you and I who are victimized by this special kind of madness. From time to time it happens to everybody. We all worry about our "image." Remember me at the start of the chapter? I wasn't concerned about your understanding this; I was worried about what you and others would think about me. And remember what I said later—this lesson isn't one which we learn once and are done with. We keep learning it over and over—I suspect till the end of our lives.

You'll notice that when you're writing to impress, you'll be worried that your sentences aren't long enough. You'll be concerned about them seeming immature or high-schoolish or something. You'll even say things like, "oh, that sounds dumb." Sounds. The more important you become, the more you may fall into this trap. You may find yourself using the most complicated sentences possible. You'll want to use the maximum number of words, phrases, and/or clauses in each sentence so as to ensure that each and every reader who might read it, or, for that matter, every listener to whom it might be read, is or would be—if it were the case that he is just a potential reader or listener—duly, not so say necessarily, impressed with the erudition of the writer whether or not it is the case that he (the reader or listener, that is to say) understands a word of it.

Maybe someday you'll be on some committee of faculty members from the Harvard Law School. Then you'll feel compelled to write reports that sound like this:

> **With respect to the current year we would state that although the question of restrictions on use of grades before the start of the third year remains open, there is every likelihood that a pass-fail system will not be instituted—in other words, that examinations will be graded and the grades recorded.**

Now for one thing, if you have had any doubts about your ability to use words, think in these terms: if you couldn't use words more effectively than that committee of scholars, you would have starved to death by now.

If you can answer the question "What does the passage mean?" you probably can say it more clearly. That simply means that you probably can communicate better than that bunch of Harvard Law School professors.

Why in the world do you suppose that they write so that nobody can understand them? Well, they don't try not to be understood, actually. What happens is that they get so wrapped up in *sounding* like a bunch of high-class scholars that they just plain forget that the point of saying something is to be understood—so they end up sounding high class, all right. And communication? It's not attacked—it's just ignored—and it doesn't happen.

Think now about how this problem affects you. When you write, are you concerned with how you sound? How about when you talk? When you talk to an "important" person, do you try to be careful to speak right? When you write, do you find you worry about how the piece will sound? Do you find yourself agonizing over the difference between "lie" and "lay"? Do you find yourself stopping in midsentence to scurry off to the dictionary or usage handbook to find out whether it's "I seen" or "I saw"? When you mean "city" do you want to say "municipality"? Instead of "first," does "initial" seem more impressive? Do you worry over "he doesn't" or "he don't"? And really mean "he does"? That's what happens many times and that's why being worried over how it sounds is impractical.

 Discuss: Can you remember being concerned with your image and falling flat on your face? Perhaps you'd rather recall such a story about somebody else instead of yourself. After you've dis-

cussed the problem write about it. After you've finished writing get into groups and read your stories to one another.

NOVEMBER 27

Arran Smith's journal entry about his ''image.''

''Your friendly neighborhood Spiderman''

I was 13 and in the sixth grade when I had this craze to be a Super hero. I loved them all, especially the ones seen in marvel magazines. There was Dr. Bruce Banner who turned into the ''Hulk'' a 7 foot 1,000 pound monster when angered. Capt. America a soldier who was a 98 lb weakling until a scientific formula transformed him into America's super solider.

But the only hero I felt I could really relate to was Spiderman, alias Peter Parker, bitten by a radioactive spider, enabling him to climb walls and giving him more than normal strength. So one evening I decided I would become Spiderman. I drew a spider on the front and back of my T-shirt, I put on long underwear and a brown papersack over my head.

Then I snuck out the house through the backdoor. I saw some kids down the street in front of the Fire Station. I yelled, ''Hey you kids, leave that firestation alone!'' They turned around to see me in my ridiculous get up, and they chased me. I ran back down to the house and entered into the backdoor before they could see where I vanished.

At the time of my Spiderman craze I was attending the Attucks Grammar School. Some of the kids who had chased me attended the same school. One in particular, Jesse Talley. The next morning at school there was no small gossip about last evenings spectacular event. Jesse said to me, ''Hey Arran, there was a Super Hero

on your block last night. Did you see him?'' I
said yes. I felt like Clark Kent with my double
identity.
      Later that night I put on my costume and
scanned Hickory once more. This time the kids
were waiting for me. When I went around the
corner they were lurking in a garageway. All of
a sudden they leaped out saying ''Ha Ha we got
em, let's unmask him.'' I was filled with fear
thinking of how I would be disgraced and
humiliated when the kids unmasked me. Finally I
said, ''Jesse, I thought you were my friend.''
Jesse lifted the paperbag over my head and
laughed, ''it's Arran, so you're the Spider
Man.'' Embarrassment burned my cheeks. I said
goodnight turned and went home and tore up all
my comics.

                                           END

NOVEMBER 28

      Here's another of Don Hensley's pieces.

           HE LET HIS LIFE POST TOASTEE

Yes, and I've tried to capture you before

and how your presence escapes me!

You laugh but ache to cry

hiding under a mound of plastic polished
disguises

The stirring wind carries your memories,

drifting evermore away from you -

better run to catch up!

lose no time in grasping for the cause.

You've made your moves,

172

down through the years

Now look at your glassy eyed frown

against a deep pool of tears

dripping motionless off the mountain's edge,

splashing onto a plateau of frozen lies,

distilled there forever.

And now there's nothing left, but the stain on
the linen,

still damp from this mornings slashed arms –

curiously strung out disjoint;

across the bedrooms' dusty floor.

Chapter XVII

By now you've faced many of the problems with words in a very concrete way. Think of the problems that make using words to communicate a hopelessly naive notion:

(1) You have your own unique vocabulary, and while it helps lots to put the words into sentences, the sentences are made of words anyway.

(2) Not only is your vocabulary different from your listener's, but they're both changing constantly.

(3) Not only are the vocabularies changing, but you and your listener are changing so that it's hard to decide who you're communicating to—to say nothing of how hard it is to decide who you are.

Which brings us back to a basic consideration—why even try to communicate? I'm sure you came up with lots of reasons before.

But sometimes when we use words it's unimportant whether we're communicating. We use words simply to record ourselves. Sometimes we use words when nobody is around, when nobody is there to understand, or be impressed or like us or anything. Last night I was going to the icebox to get a glass of milk. I had left a chair in the middle of the room. It was dark; my toe hit the chair and I hurt and felt the need to say something—no one was there, but there I was making words come out just as though I was communicating. What I was doing was taking my anger out on myself and putting it into sounds which were outside of me; there I could hear my anger—even, in a peculiar way, enjoy it. I was making it into an object.

This use of language is related to the problems we have with the way we change so fast. You see, with the way we're changing so fast and so constantly, and since it's so hard for us to decide who and what we are, we're fascinated with ourselves. If we'd stay the same all the time, we'd get bored with ourselves; but, of course, we are constantly checking up on ourselves, checking ourselves out.

Watch people (even yourself!) trying on clothes. They're not really checking out the clothes . . . in the mirror for all that time. At least I'm not. I'm looking at me. How does my hair look from this side if I turn so? Not too bad if I move my head this way, etc., etc., etc. Or did you ever notice people walking past department store windows? Those windows make beautiful mirrors, don't they? I can check to see how this jacket goes with these pants as I walk downtown. Do these shoes make my feet look too big with these slacks?

Vanity, you say. Well, call it whatever you want to, but most of us find ourselves fascinating.

I want you to take a picture of me at the zoo. While I'm eating my birthday cake. Or take one just at the moment I get married. And I want to see them as soon as they get developed—in fact I can't wait to see how the pictures turn out. (They developed the Polaroid so none of us has to wait.) I really enjoy going through the pictures of myself as a little boy, climbing on my grandpa's porch, sitting on the marble lion at the zoo, being pulled on my sled by the little girl who lived up the street.

What lies behind this, it seems to me, is our need to freeze ourselves in time and space for, just like waves, we appear and disappear without even slight notice. This moment will never exist again. Poof—it's gone. But I want to cut out of the ocean of waves one moment with the one wave that is me. And I want to preserve it. And I want to look at it over and over and over.

Two things are happening: I'm fascinated by me and I try to make myself permanent somehow. Lots of us do this with writing. We just want to get ourselves down on paper to see how we look. Writing is, in this way, a kind of mirror or a self-aimed portrait camera. Let's see me as I think about what it's like to be in love, how I felt my first day in the army, or what I think of my boss who thinks he's so smart or how I look missing someone who's far away.

Surely you've had experience with this. I know I've been in love off and on now since I was a teen-ager and what I usually do a lot is write about how I feel. I used to think I was writing the letters or poems or whatever for Mary or Gretchen or Linda to read. But I now think I was really writing for me— I was looking in the mirror to see how I look in love—sort of the same as looking to see how I looked with my hair arranged this way or that. As I wrote, I was holding my hands in my back pockets, then crossing my arms; I was posing this way and that because I was interested in looking at myself and because I wanted to freeze that "me" or those various "me's" so I could look at them more.

The important thing to remember about this kind of writing is that when I do it, I'm the guy I'm trying to satisfy and I'm really not trying to communicate to anybody else. So I don't have to worry about whether anybody else will understand what I'm saying. All I'm doing is posing a bit and looking in the mirror. I could, for example, say "That class is like one great big brown leather armchair," and move on to discuss (with myself) what I was doing at the zoo on my birthday. I wouldn't have to worry about anybody understanding what that stuff about the chair is all about.

Choose something important to you—something really important, like falling in love last week, or what you felt when somebody close to you died, or what you really think of your best friend, or what you'd really like to be doing right now. Or what happened to you when you were embarrased by your own clumsiness. Or what makes you happy. Or what you'd really like to be doing right now. Or how it feels to finish doing something you really like to do. Or what you really like to do. Write it. For you.

When you've finished decide what kind of person wrote this. Does what you wrote look like what you wanted it to? Do you want to change it? Why? Or, I suppose, why not? Do it your way, for you, about you, until it pleases you. When it pleases you, it's done. Now you know what God felt like on the seventh day when he was pleased and said: "It is good." And you can rest.

NOVEMBER 29

Both Trudy Robinson and Ralph Williams read to the class tonight: Trudy about an embarrassing experience when she was very young and Ralph about coming to know his son.

''A Second Grade Experience''
by Truephania Robinson

It was about the last of November of my second grade school year. In that class Mary Robinson and I just happen to be the ''teacher's pets.'' The teacher came in that day as usual assigning, more or less, chores to us. Mary was told to clean out the case which contained paper, pencils, crayon, ec. I was told to go and ask the custodian for a bucket and put some water in it. When I returned to the classroom she put some dishwashing liquid in the bucket that she keeps in her drawer -of-personals. She then handed me a pair of scissors, I guess at that point I was standing in a spot where most

of the eyeballs of the class could see me,
looking pretty much uninformed. She reached into
her drawer-of-personals again and took out about
four large peanut butter jars and she told me to
put the peanut butter jars in the water and let
the labels soak and then take the scissors and
scratch them off. Suddenly all my classmates
began snickering, I felt like she had just told
a joke using me as a subject. Ignoring the
classmates, I thought well, this is easy enough
but, I was in for a shock. I also knew that she
had confidence in me, she knew that I would do
the job well, but she too had started scraping,
the loose parts of the paper fell right off, but
the parts that were attached directly to the
glue didn't come off by my hands being smaller
than the scissors didn't help.

I continued scraping while frustration
builded up inside of me, tears began to fall
from my eyes until I just cried out. All the
students looked up with their mouths open and
their eyes not blinking as if they had just saw
a ghost. The teacher ran over to me with a
puzzling face shouting what's wrong. At the
time, being the main attraction, I couldn't say
nothing I just cried more and more.

She grabbed me and took me down to the
nurse's office and they both tried to find out
why I was crying. Knowing that I couldn't get
the label off the jar, I had to think of a quick
lie. So, I told them that my stomach was
hurting. The nurse popped another fast question,
one that I didn't expect, of course. ''What did
you eat for breakfast?'' Being young and stupid
I thought stomach aches only came from eating
bad food, so I told another quick lie. I said,
''I had some leftover Turnip Greens that had
been setting up overnight, candy, and cookies.''
They both turned their lips down, I thought to
myself that must be a good one. The teacher
suddenly rushed out of the nurse's office, I

thought she must have been going to puke. The nurse told me to have a seat. I sat down with a witty smile knowing I had just got over.

I sat there ten maybe fifteen minutes then my heart nearly stopped when I saw my mother walk in with my teacher. I believe the teacher had already informed her of what had happened because she didn't ask any questions, she just took me home. As soon as we got in the house she asked me, ''Why did you?'' I stood there speechless and then bursted out with tears being her baby she just patted me up and told me not to worry about it.

I thought it was all the teacher's fault and I tried to think of a way to get her back. But, before I knew it I fell asleep and I dreamed. I dreamed it was the last day of school before Christmas break and that that was the day I had planned to get my revenge. After school that day I saw her on the way to her car. I threw a brick at her and it hit her in the head. She fell on the sidewalk and bumped her head on the curve. People suddenly started crowding around including the principal. Somebody called the ambulance and they took her away on the stretcher. She seemed to be in a deep sleep. Later the news got to my mother that she was in the hospital in a coma: My mother told me that she was in a coma and she explained to me what that meant and that it was a possibility of her not coming out. I was kind of scared because I thought I had injured her badder than I had intended.

On the following day another teacher came by my house and brought me a Christmas present from her. I opened it and it was a sweater. I started crying. I felt like a fool. My mother entered the room where I was and I suddenly dried my eyes and showed her what the teacher had gave me and she said she would take me to the hospital later so that I could thank her.

At the hospital, she managed to sneak me in. After she saw her in her room, she told me she would wait outside the door for me. Once she left I started crying because I was so guilty that I didn't know where to begin. I started by thanking her for the sweater and telling her how much I liked it, I went on to tell her that she was a nice person, and a nice teacher, and finally I told her that I liked her and that never gave a teacher an apple before but I was going to give her one when school starts back, by this time I was crying so hard that I couldn't say any more.

I began running toward the door when I felt somebody shaking me, it was my mother. My eyes were full of tears when I woke, she asked me why was I crying, I was tempting to tell her that my stomach was hurting but instead I told her that I had had a bad dream because I was a big cry baby.

My Son
by Ralph Williams

My son came home from Atlanta to spend the weekend. I picked him up at the airport friday afternoon. Boy was I surprised to see how much he has grown in so short of time. He's almost as tall as I am, in fact, he's just about at my shoulder. And what's worse he can now wear my clothes quite well. Which is really going to present a problem this summer. It really shouldn't be too much trouble though, because at the rate he's growing he'll pass me up this summer. The main thing is I enjoyed him the weekend. I guess I must miss having him around. He made me feel very proud the way he conducted himself while here. I was previously invited to go to a concert saturday night at the Kiel Opera House. Since he had conducted himself so nicely. I decided to get him a ticket and take him along. He seem to have enjoyed himself. I think the real reason he did so, was because I more or less let out on his own. Oh by the way his name is Tony and he's everyday of thirteen, and he thinks he's as old as I. Anyway I was able to buy his ticket in the same row I was sitting in about five seats down, he took his girl friend with him and I think it gave him a sense of independence. It doesn't seem like me or maybe to him too, but he acted as if it did. This was really the first time I've actually taken him to a social function such as this. And I know what goes on out there in the audience while the lights goes out, because I'm only sixteen years older than he. So I know some of the things that kids do today for entertainment. I'm just hoping that some of those talks I've been giving him, is paying off. Anyway everyone enjoyed the concert. Afterwards I invited everyone for a late dinner before retiring for the night. After dropping the two girls off, my son and I talked on the way home, about everything and I learned alot from this, I only hope he picked up on some of the things we discussed. In all the weekend my son and I spent together was quite pleasing. He's finally growing up. Sometimes I wonder did my father feel the same way about me and my brothers. I'm sure he did, from the way that he raised us. My father was a good man, and I'm glad my son and father had a chance to enlighten each other. I'm sure Tony learned alot from his grandfather, because he would spend alot of time with him. In fact up until Tony was about eleven years old, his grandparents was the only parents he knew. They really did one hell of a job raising him. During the time he was very small I was working out of town and traveling alot. At that time I was singing with a religionist group touring the coast or anywhere else we could pick up some money and I was still very young myself and hadn't made up my mind on what I wanted to do with life. So sometimes I didn't see him except once or twice a year. I'm pretty sure it was a long time before he could think me or accept me as his father. In fact, once he told me, that he had always thought of me as an older brother, even though my parents had told him, I was actually his father.

At least now, that he's older, he finally realizes who I am.

NOVEMBER 30

Don Hensley wrote this piece the other day:

''JUST A THOUGHT''

Winter time comes

just a little too fast

Summer just flies by

only patiently

I'm just a fool

for yesterdays

I spend most of my nights

looking back through the haze

Chapter XVIII

I am going to share some of my writing with you. I hope that in sharing it I'm also sharing the idea. But when I wrote it—that's important—*when I wrote it,* I had only the idea in mind. I wanted to put the idea down, in words, to satisfy me, so that I could say "That's it; that's the way I feel, that's what I think." I wasn't even considering your possible existence. It was for me that I did it; it was driven out of me, I suppose, by the same force that had me screaming when I banged my toe against the chair last night. I just wanted to get me out in the open where I could experience me.

Jan. 7, 1968—Nov. 10, 1976

25 degrees below Wisconsin Winter zero
Star filled sky forever dark blue
Silent clear Night.

Inside the restaurant
The fireplace   the orange fire cuddles us
In our mothers' hugs

The candles' warm light flicks against your hair
And on the red wool dress.
The fire's speckles on your smile
Move
They reach across the table to me
That smile connects us we touch with it

We are inside a Xmas tree

Inside

When we met in the hall last night
You were wearing that red dress.
The hem is altered.

I guess styles change.

But now I've shown it to you. And a different force starts working on me.

I find that the minute I showed it to you I felt a need to explain it—to tell what I had in mind, or where I was, and all that. That's because the minute I share my expressions with others, they turn into communications. Now one of my expressions came out in the above form, maybe yours came out in a different form, but no matter how they turned out, I'm sure that they had this in common—the minute you showed yours to someone else, you felt the urge to explain.

 Discuss: Why the need to change what already was satisfactory? If you were to change what you wrote, why would it take starting from scratch? Or would it take starting from scratch?

Let me give you an example of changing from pure expression to sharing expression. Sometimes I do not use words to express myself. Sometimes, I sing (in the bathtub, usually), sometimes I cook—I make, for instance, a ground veal recipe that I invented.

Well I didn't really invent it, I dreamt it. Literally. I woke up one morning with this recipe in my head. So I wrote it down, and that night I made it for myself. It was lovely: brown crisp crust on an oblong meat patty set off by the color of the topping—green onions, yellow melted butter, and brown fried mushrooms. And the flavor—first the wine and butter put a layer of flavor all over the inside of my mouth; this flavor was just tickled by an occasional bit of dill as the meat got chewed. While I was chewing it, the garlic and mushroom melted through the butter-wine layer in the front of my mouth. Soon the veal and onion flavors gently breathed away the layer in the middle of my mouth. Then the lemon flavor glided through the rest of the wine and butter in the back of my mouth.

Here's how I made it.

Ingredients:

½ lb. ground veal
2 shots worcestershire sauce
pinch cayenne pepper
pinch salt
¼ tsp. dry hot mustard
½ pinch dill weed

1 egg
1 tbsp. red wine
juice from ¼ lemon

⅛ lb. butter
5 mushrooms, sliced
juice from ¼ lemon

three green onions, chopped
1 clove garlic, chopped fine
3 tbsp. red wine

rye bread crumbs

Mix the stuff from the first group in a bowl. Form it into two 1-inch-thick oblong patties. Mix stuff from the second group in a flat dish. Ignore these two parts for a bit. Melt butter in a small skillet. Add mushrooms and garlic. When mushrooms begin to brown, add lemon. Now dip meat in egg-wine mixture. When it is just about finished, add onions and wine.

Now this tasted so good that I made it again and invited friends in to share it. In fact I just shared it with you. Why? Because, like most people, I am not usually satisfied with keeping things to myself. It's the same as when you hear a joke that you haven't heard before. What's your first instinct? I know mine is to search out a friend to tell him the joke. We seem to be sharing creatures— some things are just too good to keep to ourselves. We want to share ourselves with each other—even writing a recipe is an act of sharing—and that's what communication is.

 Think about your favorite joke. It's good to share. You've got something that is simply too good to keep to yourself. Recall Marion and her theory about communication and sharing? Well, go ahead and give your joke to somebody: write it down and give it away.

Here's one old one I've always liked.

A couple, married for five years, had lived happily together for all that time, enjoying, most of all, sex.

The husband always came home from the office looking forward to jumping into the sack with his wife and romping around for an hour or two before dinner. Then, after dinner, he looked forward to going back to the bedroom, soon to be joined by his wife.

This went on year after year.

One night the husband came home and ran into the bedroom to meet his wife.

They ripped the covers back on the bed and began but nothing happened and finally they go so tired and full of sweat that they both gave up.

After dinner they rested awhile, watched television, and then, with a sense of desperation, they headed back to the bedroom, only to wear themselves out again.

And that night she didn't sleep. And, although he was very tired, neither did he.

And this went on the next night and the night after that, until one night during dinner she just turned to him and said,

"Dear, I think you ought to see a physician."

He looked at her incredulously.

"Or I ought to," she said.

He forces a smile. "I'll go," he said, with very grim determination.

And so the next day he went, and the doctor examined him and pronounced him to be a sound physical specimen.

"The only thing is, you're wearing yourself out," the doctor said. "You've overdone it." He began to write out a prescription and then tore it up. He looked at his long-suffering patient. "The thing I'm going to prescribe for you is difficult, but you're strong and young and seem to have plenty of will-power. You must abstain from all relations for one month."

"One month?" the man said.

"That's right," the doctor said. "You'll find that it will be worth it."

And, head hanging, the man left the doctor's office and went home to tell his wife about the "prescription," and she wanted to know if it applied to her, and he said "You bet it does" in a voice that left no doubt.

That was the first day. And they got through the next day. Then the next week, and he took up smoking and she spent the day lazing around the house watching the "soaps" on TV, and then they took up movies, and finally, when he was smoking four packs a day, he went back to see the doctor to see if there wasn't some way the sentence could be lightened.

The doctor said that he had lasted almost two whole weeks, and if he could do that, he could last two weeks longer, and what's more, he could cut down on smoking.

But he kept smoking, and she kept watching the soaps, and she started going to matinee movies, and he took up the Royal Canadian Exercises, and they had friends on for bridge a lot, and ordered a stag movie from Denmark.

But, with a week to go, he found himself becoming increasingly nervous and his teeth had all turned yellow from excessive smoking and he couldn't concentrate on his job at all.

"I can't keep this up," he told the doctor. "All I can think about is my wife." He began to plead with the doctor. "I can't stand it! Release me from that horrible sentence."

"This is not a sentence," the doctor explained. (After all, it wasn't the doctor who was suffering.) "This is an instruction—for your own good!"

The patient tended not to believe anybody who did something for "his own good," and he told the doctor.

"You have only one week to go," the doctor said. "If you need to smoke, you can smoke. Take up chewing gum, too. And watch that stag movie, if you must."

"I'll try," the young man said, defeated. He walked toward the door. "I'll try." He opened the door to leave. "Damn it! I'll try." He left the office, and, for the first time in years, he was nearly crying.

He told his wife, who had taken to eating chocolates in large quantities and had joined the volleyball team at the YWCA.

And the days passed, slowly, and more slowly, until five days later, he found himself back in the waiting room of the doctor's office, not smoking at all, and with a broad smile across his lips.

"Come in," the doctor said, smiling back at him. "What happened?"

"I'm so embarrassed," he said. "I really tried."

"But with just two days to go you couldn't make it?" the doctor said.

"That's right."

"Tell me," the doctor said, in a very professional tone, "How did it happen?"

"Well, my wife and I were eating dinner together. And she passed the mashed potatoes and I passed her the meat and we looked at each other and we got so hungry for one another that we pushed the table clear—knives, forks, spoons, mashed potatoes, celery, everything went right onto the floor and we jumped up onto the surface of the table ourselves, and right then and there . . ."

"You did it?" the doctor said.

"That's right," he said. "We did it."

The doctor lit a cigarette. "Tell me," he said, in *that* same professional tone. "How was it?"

"Fine," the young man said, smiling broadly. He got up, and then turned back and smiled as he opened the door. "Of course, we'll never be able to eat at Howard Johnson's again."

Chapter XIX

When we communicate we are not merely sharing ideas, or recipes, we are offering gifts. And, like when we offer other gifts, when we offer a word-gift we offer a part of ourselves.

A couple of years ago, a friend and I worked at a summer camp for kids from Los Angeles who ordinarily wouldn't have had the money to go to summer camp. Their parents would send a dollar or so with each kid so he or she could buy candy bars or something at the camp store. Linda and I were sitting with some of the boys and girls after supper one night. Linda, who was trying to quit smoking at the time, was wishing she had a cigarette. One of the boys, Phillip (eight years old) was especially attentive to Linda because he had a crush on her. When he asked her why she didn't have a cigarette, she told him that she was broke. Phillip disappeared for a few minutes, soon to return with a fifty-cent piece—the end of his candy money.

Linda didn't want to take the money, but she did—and rightly so, I believe. He wasn't offering just a few cents or even his whole fortune; he was offering a part of himself. By rejecting his gift, Linda would have been rejecting Phillip, the giver; she would have been saying no to a part of a human being. Have you ever had a present rejected? If you have, you know how bad you feel in a case like that. That's why, when friends liked a meal I made they are affirming; they are enjoying an aspect of me—my cooking. So when they like it, I am glad.

The important point is, of course, that these word-gifts are very much a part of us. One of the big difficulties of writing in school is that the person who's about to read our work is usually trained to attack; we feel very insecure turning over a part of ourselves to a trained executioner, so we try to hide ourselves by keeping ourselves out of what we write in school.

Now, when I share my joke or my idea of what a pretty girl is or my recipe, I'm sharing myself. The ideas shared are as much a part of me as the hands I'm using to write with, so I'm really sharing Dick. A problem: in school, the person I'm writing for is many times a trained butcher whose job is to see what's wrong with what I say, to tear me and my ideas down.

So I try to escape the sharp red pencil. I keep me out of my writing; since I'm a bit insecure about turning over a part of myself to a trained executioner, I write about clouds and what's "important"—to everybody but me.

But it isn't just in school that we keep ourselves out of our writing. In business letters, in letters of job application, in almost every kind of writing—

even letters to friends—we fear to display ourselves. No, it isn't just in the classroom that we have this fear and it isn't just the teacher we're afraid of.

The following could never have been written if the author had anything in mind but sharing herself. Remember my daughter Julie telling about Larry and me? Just like Julie, Angela gives us part of herself, shares herself with us. Angela's poem:

Sea-Gods

Your hair is full of gulls,
My love,
Its golden madness gloried by the wind
I see them flying
birds and all the sky
pulled by your beauty
into a fearsome circle
that I can enter only by my awe

These birds have touched your watery spirit
and guard your ocean soul

Land-locked,
I am left to marvel at such airy force.

One of my students, Judy Ross, brought me this next one. It's what she understood her grief to be. She hadn't tried to write anything fancy; she didn't want a bunch of fake school stuff for this moment. She just opened herself up and put down what a particular moment meant to her, her definition.

O, my daughter lies dead in the night, and I watch her
Her corpse must be guarded from vandals and thieves
The moonlight brings ghosts to her side, and I watch her.
The Devil lurks there in a bank of black leaves.
Watching my daughter, and I watch the Devil,
Knowing my soul is the corpse that he seeks.
My daughter lies dead, and I'm still her mother.
The moonlight shines on all,
Its water-light leaks over my face, upturned and cold.
Lifeless as I, who watch,
And She, Queen of Corpses,
Who watches over me.

Now Judy is not a "professional" writer. In fact she's in a special program here at Forest Park for students who have dropped out of school. She's an eighteen-year-old human being who went through a terrible experience and absorbed it. The big difference between her and many others is that she wrote out of herself. She was not afraid to put herself down on paper for somebody else to see and understand.

I've shown you enough of other people cutting out pieces of their lives and sharing them. Perhaps I should do the same. O.K. Perhaps the most memorable moment of this year for me was the death of my Mother. I can't think of any moment that would be closer to me, anything that would be more likely to expose me more.

So here is that moment cut out from my life and frozen—written to share myself with you:

Ma is in her coffin—but not "hers" really, cause she's dead and can't have anything anymore cause she's not anymore. I'm trying to get my head around that—trying to understand it—struggling to get that unchangeable fact inside me.

I look at the shoulders that were inside the brown corduroy coat the last time I saw her—cold dark night, dark green car she's getting into, light from my sister's house shining from behind me and on her. I give her a little kiss and hug and I feel those shoulders so thin all of a sudden poking at the flesh on my upper arms. God she's lost weight—even her smile isn't as chubby. When I close the car door, and Dad closes the one on his side, the inside car light goes out. She opens the window (just a little—she's afraid of catching cold with her bad heart). Car starts. Dad starts to back up.

"Bye, Dick," from the crack in the window. "Bye, Ma."

Her fingers look like wax—not like the strong fleshy hands I held the afternoon of her heart attack three years ago. My sister had called me and said I should come right down. I remember driving from Wisconsin thinking about how she had affected my life—spent hours with me telling me about how Uncle Vince had stood up under the two-flanked attack of family and tradition to leave his home town. Every hero she put in front of me did the same: somebody would say, "You can't do such and such; what will people say?" He'd answer, "Tough, I have to live my own life."

Then I walked into the hospital room. She was lying on the bed and I took her hands and bent down and kissed her. "Hi, Ma." She was all doped up and punchy, but she opened her eyes and looked at my beard.

(Since I had just grown it that summer, she had never see it.) She never even said "Hi," or "How're the kids?" or anything. She just whispered up "Dick, don't let them make you shave your beard."

Now she's dead. She's not there. She's not anywhere. She's not. I can't know that. I'm trying but I can't absorb it.

Now I hear the stuff people are saying at the wake: "She looks fine, better than she has for years." (Goddammit. Nobody looks better dead than alive. Look at those plastic hands.) "She's happier now." (Shut up with that talk; she's not happy or sad; she's dead—she isn't anything now.) I kept hearing all that funeral talk I've been laughing at for years in novels. Only it's not so funny now; it's infuriating. I want to grab hold of people and shake them, but I know the struggle I'm really having is with me.

(I'm trying, Ma—idiot, she's not there. You're as crazy as anybody else.)

Maybe the flowers tell it all as well as anything else. Inside the coffin is a heart-shaped white bouquet—about a foot long with a banner that says "grandma."

Some relatives of my Ma's came from out of town. They sit right behind me talking about the grandchildren's flowers. He decided that if he "went first," he'd like a white bouquet like that and she'd like a red one.

On the bottom half of the coffin red roses with a red ribbon which says "wife, mother." All around are big displays from my Dad's union, from Ma's sister, from Dad's family, from a whole variety of friends and relatives who came to look at the corpse and be afraid they'd be next.

Pretty flowers, pretty words but they all miss Ma's toughness.

She went through World War II raising two kids because her husband was drafted. After the war she saw her husband through an incredible series of unlucky accidents and illnesses—nearly one a year. Factory nearly cuts his finger off one year. Then he gets diabetes and finds it nearly impossible to balance his diet and his insulin. As a result Dad was constantly in danger of insulin shock—which Ma had to struggle with many times. Then his appendectomy.

Last year Dad had an operation for gall bladder. Ma had been getting weaker as her heart was evidently deteriorating. I pushed her down the hall of the hospital in a wheel chair to see Dad the day after the operation. She hated the weakness that everybody could see: her in her wheelchair. God, she bristled. Really hated it.

All of a sudden, as I'm writing this, I understand part of why that whole funeral scene drove me mad. Ma never wanted pity; she would do anything to keep from showing weakness. She was too proud to accept a situation where someone was superior to her. Another thing she couldn't stand was self-pity. So there we all were—first, feeling sorry for ourselves; for our own deaths which her death reminded us of and for our loss of her; and second, feeling sorry for her.

And she was dead and couldn't defend herself from it all.

Then, on the afternoon before the funeral, David's flowers came. David only met Ma once last summer, but I guess I talk a lot about her, so he knew her fairly well. That's probably why he could say something real in the midst of all the unreal. His flowers were pure white and not such a splashy huge display. I walked over to look at the card. "Deepest grief for the death of a courageous woman."

That's mine. As I read it I'm startled and a bit embarrassed by the arrogance that runs through it; it's like I'm the only one who was right about Ma and the whole situation. When I write down what's really inside me, I understand me a bit better. That's what some teachers mean by "writing to objectify experience for self-understanding." What it means is that writing is a mirror, a good one if you don't pose too much.

But I used the piece here because just looking in the mirror isn't sufficient. I want you to understand me, or at least I want to tell you about me so you could understand me if you wanted. I can hear someone objecting. "Hey. That wasn't about you. It was about your mother. The way you're talking, it was about you." O.K. Fair objection.

But here's the way I see it. What you read was my explanation of what my mother's death *meant* to me, sort of my definition of the event.

To do that I had to make you live through the event as close to the way I did as possible. Plus I had to look fairly closely at the background that helped shape it for me. I tried to make it possible for you to experience that moment as I did. And I did it by opening myself, by passing on to you the experiences (or at least as many as seemed necessary) that went into making that moment "mean" to me what it did.

Once I realize that, I understand why I was uneasy about how I came off in my story. I feel the temptation to go back and rewrite it so I seem more humble. "Maybe if I. . ." I keep thinking. But I'm not going to. Too bad if you don't like me. My only job was to write so you could understand me.

I think that it might be useful for me to share not only this piece but the writing of it. I'm going to try to show you the piece getting written; I'm going to try to share with you what I went through as I wrote it, what went hard and what didn't. Also what it felt like to be done.

Writing that piece cost me; it was hard. I don't mean that it was hard to figure out how to write it, nor do I mean I had to wonder what to say. These problems were a breeze. No, the difficulty was in facing my subject; it was one I didn't want to look at, didn't want to face. But most important of all, perhaps, is that as long as it was just a memory, it could seem unreal. But as soon as I made it into a concrete piece of writing, it would lose its unreality. So like most people, I suppose, I put off the unhappy; and, also like most people, I found out that even putting off comes to an end.

I sat here in my apartment for two days, a Friday and a Saturday, with paper in front of me and a pen in my hand. Put on a record. Listen to it for a while. Get up and turn it off. "Gonna get to work now." Back up to make a sandwich first, though. Flip on the TV. Wash a few dishes. Read an old magazine. Glass of milk—no, let's have an eggnog. Back to the paper and pen.

I'm bored. Maybe my daughter Lisa would like to go to a show. "Want to go to a movie?"

"No, you've got your writing to do, don't you?"

"Yeah, but that's O.K. You have to go back home tomorrow. Let's catch a flick."

So off to the movies.

But it's no good. All that I can think of are lines and approaches that I might use when I write about Ma. I've got to get after that piece of writing. Not because of a deadline, not because anybody is forcing me, not because of anything, but I've got this thing I have to do. A part of me had got to get written.

Sunday morning comes and the Sunday papers. I read as much and as slowly as I can. Funnies, sports page, women's section, picture section. In desperation I read even the news and editorial sections. Finally, there is no way out. Got to write.

I knew what it was going to be about; I knew what I wanted to say. It had to do with the memory of my mother. She had died about two months before and I really wanted to isolate and record the emotion I had; I wanted just to get it down so I could see it once and for all. And I wanted to get down with enough information so that when I showed it to somebody else, they might share. They might "understand."

So, I took a deep breath and started writing. I tried to choose the pictures that stayed in my head and let my pen write down the thoughts as they came. For example, the first paragraph went down as fast as my pen would move:

Ma is in her coffin—but not "hers" really, cause she's dead and can't have anything anymore cause she's not anymore. I'm trying to get my head around that—trying to understand it—struggling to get that unchangeable fact inside me.

I tried to figure out what the whole experience "meant" to me—what were the objects, what were the thoughts that added up to the whole experience. As I felt this particular way, what was I thinking about, what was I remembering? I tried to find those objects and ideas which added up for me, and I blindly hoped that they would add up the same way for my reader.

The point here is what I looked for were *things*: hands, colors, events. If I chose honestly, the things added up to a part of me. And if you and I have much in common, then you'll understand that part of me. Perhaps that commonness is what constitutes our humanity. (And perhaps there is no such commonality.)

I said I had to choose honestly. By that I mean that I had to choose the objects and events and thoughts that were really there in my mind. Not the ones I wished were there. And just as I had to choose the details honestly, I had to write honestly. I had to let it come out the way it came out and I had to let it be me, and then write it like that. I couldn't worry about how it would sound; I couldn't let the tempation to remake myself distract me from the real job.

This latter is not so simple as it might seem. I constantly found myself slowing up my writing to think of something clever, or to delete something I was afraid would sound stupid. Again, it's evidently a lifelong struggle.

If communication occurs, my readers will have similar events stirred in them; my writing will strike a part of them that they'll want to share. They could, of course, notice the neat way I say things, or they could remember reading something like this, but then all they'd be experiencing is my writing—and not *what* I'm writing about—in this case the feeling I have about my mother's death and all that it means.

I'm not sure that's at all clear, so I'll go at it another way. Let's say you take a picture of your new baby daughter to show it to your friends so they can understand part of what she "means" to you. They look at it and say, "Gee, that camera takes good pictures," or "Say, you're really a good photographer," or "Look at the clear focus—you can see every hair." But you wanted them to see how pretty little Ursula is, or what a funny smile she has, or what a bright sparkle she has in her eyes. They'd have only experienced your photography, not *what* you photographed.

The ultimate confirmation that you've communicated, the response that tells you as surely as you can be told that your message got across, is when somebody pulls out a picture of his own kid and says, "They look like they'd get into the same trouble, don't they?" or "I bet they'd be friends," or something like that. If you agree, you can be fairly certain you've communicated.

When I write something, I'm really pleased when somebody points to an essay, or picture, or a story that s/he is reminded of by what I've written. I'm most pleased of all if somebody reads my writing and says, "That's how I felt when I. . ." and then goes on to tell me something from his or her own life which I recognize as like what I've been trying to communicate.

 Discuss: I said before that while I only seem to be writing about my mother, what I'm really writing about is me. Now, is there really any difference? That is, when I'm writing about me, am I really writing about you and me and all humans? Is this what "communication" means? Is this what "communication" depends on? If you find out an answer to any of these questions, please stop everything and write to me immediately.

You've now had a good number of examples of people allowing themselves to share themselves.

Take some aspect of you and your own life and write about it. A receipe? Maybe. A poem? A moment from your own life when you were ecstatic? or grief-stricken? Perhaps. An idea you have for a career? Your understanding of your love for a child? How it feels to fix an auto engine and hear it sound just right? Copy these pieces on a ditto master. Then give everybody in the class one copy of each person's work. Each of you now has a book of things which are important.

DECEMBER 1

One member of the class, Ray Henn, is an apprentice meat cutter with a supermarket chain. For the first half of the semester he wrote in his journal about his job: from the power structure in the various stores to which he has been assigned to how to prepare various cuts of meat. A few weeks ago, he said that he had done enough writing about how to do things and how things worked and wanted to try to write about feelings. This is what he wrote.

Now I would like to write a little about my father who died two years ago. When I look back on my childhood and then look around me at the present, I realize how good of a father my father really was. I sort of resent my father getting up in years when I was still pretty young, though.

He married my mother when he was about
thirty-four years old. Growing up on a farm near
Decatur, Illinois, in the early part of the
century didn't require much schooling, so he
only went through sixth grade. He came from a
family of ten children and they were a pretty
close family. After he left the farm and moved
to Saint Louis to get a job, he and his sister,
my Aunt Rose, went back home to visit very
often. It really sounded like a fun time. They
would take their friends whom they met in St.
Louis home with them on weekends. These little
weekend visits were never ''little'' by the time
the ten children brought their friends and wives
and families along, but I see pictures of these
get-togethers and the people really seemed to
enjoy themselves.

My father worked in an ammunitions plant
during World War II and so did my mother, who
just happened to be friends with my Aunt Rose. I
think the first time my mother started taking my
father seriously was on Armistice Day. After
work the group decided to all meet at a
particular bar. Well, my mother drinks maybe one
beer a year, and she really didn't want to go,
but, what-the-heck, it was Armistice Day, so she
went along and after that started to like my
father more than just as a friend's brother.

Right around the time my parents got married
my father got an apprenticeship as a body-man.
It was really hard work in those days,
everything was done by hand, the air tools
weren't in use yet. Like any apprentice he got
stuck with all the ''shit'' jobs like sanding
cars which were to be painted. He learned his
trade well and because he was good, he was able
to move around from Chevrolet Dealer to dealer
if he didn't like the conditions at the
particular shop he was at. I think he changed
dealers three times. As in so many households in
the ''good ole days,'' my mother didn't have to
work. My father worked and brought home the

197

money, thusly providing for us, and that was how
it was supposed to be. He was a good husband and
father who gave all himself to our family. Don't
get me wrong, he wasn't a complete ''goody-
goody.'' He could use foul words as well if not
better, when he got mad, then the next guy. I
can honestly say that I can't remember my father
ever getting mad and shouting at my mother. I
can't even remember him shouting at us kids very
often. He was easy-going and low keyed, but with
just a few words or a look and occasionally a
slap, he really got his meaning across. Like I
said earlier, he gave up a lot to keep his
family happy, but he had his own little
privileges like visiting the neighborhood
tavern. He met a few of his friends there after
work and had one or two beers with them, but he
was always home by five-thirty which was when we
ate. Friday night was his ''night out with the
boys.'' This amounted to going to meet his
friends at the neighborhood bar. They had
bowling leagues which bowled on these nights.
The bowling was done on electric bowling
machines and it was done in fun, but the teams
were serious about winning. My mother said she
never remembers my father coming home drunk or
even staggering and she didn't mind him enjoying
a night with his friends. A person could hardly
qualify it as a ''night out with the boys''
seeing that he was usually home by ten.

Looking back I can appreciate how much
effort it took to come home from work, which was
a physically tiring job, and go to work on any
of the projects which he had done to the house.

He was very good with his hands. It seemed,
to me, that there was nothing he could not do
well. I am glad now that I was the youngest boy,
because I was at an age where I was old enough
to help him and not too old so as I was out
galavanting around with my friends when he took
on his biggest home improvements. These were
remodeling the kitchen and adding a family room

on to the back of our house after the porch was taken off.

Like I mentioned earlier, my father was not the most educated man, but it is amazing what he accomplished by reading on the project he was undertaking and by that knowledge gained he transformed his ideas into reality. He completely built all the cabinets to the exact measurements which they had to be. I would just sit and watch him and once in a while he would let me help.

Building the room addition was where I really got the feeling of being a ''handyman.'' Again we did everything from scratch without subcontracting one bit of the work. We did everything from laying the foundation with hand mixed concrete to roofing the room ourselves. I was old enough to really help quite a bit and my help was needed because my father was beginning to feel bad.

As good as my father was at so many things, he never got a deer or had much luck at fishing; he liked both terribly. My uncle, aunt and two cousins came down from Chicago every year for deer season for about ten or twelve years. This was always a big thrill for us kids, but I think my father got the biggest thrill. I can't descirbe the feeling that I use to get when fall, and deer season, came around. It was a mixture of the excitement from the fact that out-of-town company was at our house and also from the fact that my uncle brought all kinds of camping and hunting equipment, which I loved to investigate. Even though this was such an exciting and special time of year, that did not help my father get a deer. He kept trying until he got too sick to be able to go hunting but no luck.

His luck was not too abundant when it came to fishing either. He should have had an inkling of his future luck with fishing when he use to take my little sister and myself with him. We used to bug the hell out of him by not sitting still and wanting him to put the worms on our hooks and all kinds of other little distracting things.

Anyway, the best example of how bad his luck was when we, our whole family, decided to go to Minnesota. We were going to Minnesota, the ''Land of 10,000 Lakes'' and of Norhtern Pike, averaging two to three feet in length and gigantic, hard fighting Muskellunge and Walleye. Everyone who went to fish there caught as many as they wanted. Well, as it turned out, after we got up there we learned that the lakes didn't thaw until the last part of May, and this was the second week of June. Since the time of spawning relied on when the lakes thawed, you guessed it, the fish were spawning and they were too busy to be going after some fisherman's bait. I have to admit that we did catch a lot of fish, but they were all about half the size we were expecting. Now, in light of the fact that we were at least catching a lot of fish you may not think the trip turned out too bad. Well it didn't, but still, this was a hard worked for, once in a life trip that would have been made a lot more memorable if my father could have caught his ''big ole'' Pike.

Despite his luck at deer hunting and fishing my father was good at so many things and I learned a hell of a lot from him.

One day my father experienced pain in his chest. It wasn't very bad, but it was definitely something. My father was a person who was rarely sick and never went to a doctor, so he must have been experiencing something. He didn't know what it was for sure but he thought it might have been indigestion.

He went to see a doctor after he kept experiencing this, well the more I try to remember the more I seem to recall him referring to it as a tightness in his chest rather than pain. The doctor's name was Nieman. Although it has been about twelve years ago and I was only eleven years old, I remember his name, because I don't think this guy should be allowed to practice medicine.

My father went to this ''doctor'' about his tightness and he was soon being treated for an ulcer and drinking a lot of Maalox. I could see an initial diagnosis being wrong, but this ''doctor'' treated my father for the wrong ailment for three years. This incident has really turned me against doctors, at least for anything major. I guess that is a good example of stereotyping, and I don't really mean to do that. Let me say that I will go to at least two doctors for an opinion when I really get sick.

I don't think that my father would be alive today even if that ''doctor'' had correctly diagnosed his illness right away. You see, my father had arteriosclerosis and an extra three years really wouldn't have made a difference. My father's arteries were ninety-five percent blocked when he was finally correctly diagnosed and operated on.

I don't blame his first doctor for his death. If he was operated on three years earlier he probably would have died three years earlier. I say this because the doctors gave him approximately ten years to live after the surgery, and he lived just about as long as they gave him. By saying all of this I do, I repeat, do not want to water down the fact that there are big mistakes in diagnosing illness all the time. All that doctors do is make educated guesses and a lot of times they are just plain guessing.

The treatment of the wrong illness is not so bad as the neglecting of the real problem, as in my father's case. One night after my parents had gone shopping, my father couldn't get out of the car to help carry in the groceries. His pain caused by his ''ulcer'' was treated by the method the doctor suggested, by taking Alka-

Seltzer which my mother had to bring out to the
car for him. He came through that case of
''indigestion'' which they later found out to
have been a heart attack by the bruise on his
heart when they operated. What would have
happened if my father had kept going to that
first doctor . He probably would have died from
a heart attack within a year from his first one.
If that would have been the case that doctor
would not have known how damn dumb he was. It
probably would have been said that my father's
death from a heart attack wasn't very uncommon
for such a nervous or pressured person as one
who has ulcer problems. Just to set the record
straight, my father <u>did not</u> have even a slight
ulcer, but he did have a very overworked heart
trying to pump blood through his nearly closed
arteries.

I have another gripe which is related to the
medical profession. It is called the screwed-up
hospital billing systems. The biggest screw-up
took place after my father's open heart surgery.
The hospital where the operation took place was
changing their filing system from hand filing to
computerized billing. I came from a family and
thusly a background of getting our bills paid as
quickly as they came in. Imagine this, my father
was in the hospital for I don't know how long
and a lot of that time was spent in intensive
care units, so the bill was big, putting it
mildly. Anyway, here is my poor father, weak and
feeling terrible anyway, and here comes the
bill. It was still big after Blue Cross and Blue
Shield paid their part, but it was paid in the
usual manner and we all forgot about how much it
hurt our pocket-book. The next year, quite
unexpectantly, that same bill came around again.
My parents were upset, but they figured everyone
was entitled to make one mistake. Luckily my
mother keeps her cancelled checks like people
are advised to do, for at least three years,

because those idiots at the ''new'' billing department did not have a readily available record of our payment. My mother figured a simple phone call would straighten things out, but boy was she wrong. She had to hunt up all the old forms and records of payment plus the cancelled check. Copies had to be made and a trip to the hospital had to be made to straighten out a lot of red tape. Finally, after almost flat out calling my parents liars, the paid bill was found. Then followed hurried apologies, but only about misplacing the bill, not about how impolite, impatient and just down right horse-shit they had acted throughout the whole ordeal. I would like to know what the hell they were trying to do, give my father a heart attack so they could milk us some more. It just so happened that my father didn't have any trouble due to this unnecessary stress.

Well, guess what happened the next year? Yeah, you guessed it. Those fine people screwed up again. You would think that they had learned their lesson, at least on our one particular bill, which had to be located specially for the same purpose the previous year. But no, there it was, another notice of payment due. We went through the same hassle again that year. It wound up with that hospital sending that same bill to us about four times.

The operation which we kept getting billed for was an arterial bypass, which was not a very common operation ten years ago. I think the staff may have been testing the amount of stress a patient could withstand after the operation as part of an experiment. The doctors gave my father up to ten years longer to live and he got eight out of it. I was thirteen and my little sister was ten when my father was operated on. My sister was too young to visit my father at the hospital, but I was old enough and I never went after the operation. My mother would come

home from visiting and I would either overhear
her talking to other people or I would just come
out and ask questions about him.

The descriptions I heard scared me into not
wanting to go and see him. He had an incision
from ''Adam's Apple'' to his groin for the major
surgery and there was also an incision on his
inner thigh where they took the the artery for
the by-pass from. He had I.V. tubes stuck in him
and he had tubes in his nose and also in his
incision, I think. His breast plate had to be
sawn in two so they could get his ribs pulled
apart, access to his heart. The spreading of his
rib-cage stretched and pulled all the muslces in
his upper torso so that whole area was black and
blue.

Before the operation the doctors said my
father had almost a ninety-five percent chance
to die from the operation, so this scared me. I
was thirteen at the time, but that doesn't
matter, I don't understand death any better ten
years later. Outwardly or on the surface or in
the shallow depth of my mind I feared that he
would die. Deep inside myself I really didn't
believe he would die. I guess I am a pretty
faithful person, because when I think about it I
have to say that I really believed that God
wouldn't let him die. With this in mind I, at
least, wasn't obsessed with the fear of my
father actually dying, but the thought was
always hanging in the back of my thoughts.

Like I said, I really believed that he would
be alright because God was on his side. A factor
or the factor, bigger than my belief, which
accounted for the way I sort of left the thought
of his death back in my mind, was a total
unacceptance of and unfamiliarity with the
subject of death.

I could not imagine or accept the fact that
if my father died I would no longer have a
chance to learn from him, or hear his voice or

have a person to love, just a memory. I guess I
have strong convictions because I felt the same
way eight years later when my father did die and
even as I write these words down on this paper
it is hard to think of never in regards to my
father and also in regards to the whole train of
thoughts I get when I contemplate the very term
along with its positive aspect, forever.

Chapter XX

Language is really an individual matter; each person runs around with his or her own vocabulary, never being quite sure anybody understands. Our language, you see, simply underlines our isolation from each other—we are finally alone and the separateness of our languages mirrors that loneliness.

But, as Duke Ellington said:

> Everyone is so alone—the basic, essential state of humankind; communication [is] the built-in answer to that feeling of aloneness.
>
> Communication itself is what baffles the multitude. It is both so difficult and so simple. Of all man's fears, I think men are most afraid of being what they are—in direct communication with the world at large. They fear reprisals, the most personal of which is that they "won't be understood."
>
> How can anyone expect to be understood unless he presents his thoughts with complete honesty? This situation is unfair because it asks too much of the world. In effect we say. "I don't dare show you what I am because I don't trust you for a minute, but please love me anyway because I so need you to. And of course, if you don't love me anyway, you're a dirty dog, just as I suspected, so I was right in the first place.*

The big difficulty is that the only time I write with any success is when I let myself go. The only time you have even a chance to communicate is when you take that chance. If your ideas are in your head, your words have to open up your head so your reader can see inside. Using language to communicate is a way of undressing—it's exposing yourself.

 Discuss: How are the fear of being rejected and the realization of our aloneness related? That is, would we be less afraid of rejection if we were not really alone? Or would we be less afraid of being alone if we were never concerned about being rejected? When I say that I want to be understood, you might wonder, "Does Friedrich want me to understand him or his words?" How does understanding "him" differ from understanding his words? Is there a difference? What is it? Is being "understood" in either sense a

*Duke Ellington, *Jet Magazine, May 15, 1969*

protection from being alone? Consider the following quotation from Miles Davis: "Of course you don't understand me. If you did you'd be me."

Remember the last time you were afraid? What made you afraid? What did fear feel like? Write about that fear so that you think the others in the class will understand your experience. Then divide into groups and read your papers to each other.

Discuss: Is there something which humans hold in common which makes communication? Is it common experiences? common fates? common perceptions? common feelings? common responses to the same stimuli? Do the events common to everyone (dying, mating, suffering, enjoying) shape humans into some kind of unit so that communication can occur? Are these events common to all humans? Did you ever notice that "common" and "communicate" are similar words—is there any significance to that similarity?
Is communication a myth, a hope, or reality?

DECEMBER 2

Earlier this semester, when we were doing the activity based on Dick's brown leather armchair piece, I tried to write about a ring that my grandmother had given me. I didn't include what I had written during class time because I was unhappy with it. I was unable, at the time, to gather whatever emotions I felt for my grandmother and write them.

Well, it's been very cold for the last few days, and I've been remembering that this time last year my grandmother was hospitalized for the last time. She was ninety-four and had been in a nursing home for six years, but last fall she became very ill and the staff at the home could not adequately care for her. I visited her in the hospital and watched her dying. Maybe what I was watching was her fight to stay alive even though she slept most of the time, did not seem to recognize anyone, did not talk, and could not do anything for herself.

Thinking back about her struggle and my struggle
to come to terms with her dying, I wrote this
piece.

Nana

"to me they will always be glorious birds"
<u>Harold and Maude</u>

When her tongue is green and scaly
When her leg twitches irregularly
When the nurse's aide dumps her urine into a pail
already half full
When all she can do is pick her nose

What birds will she see
What voices will she hear
What faces will she know

What will cause her head to turn
her eyes to squint
her mouth to grimace

What will keep us watching her
standing there

Hungry

Are we all caught waiting
Waiting for the birds
Those glorious birds, to cast a golden shadow on our
grief.

DECEMBER 3

I found this in Kevin's journal.

poems

are separate

poems

are continuations

                    as a breeze

                      is never

                       the same

                    though

                     moving

                       'n

                    refreshes again

                    still

                    the beauty

                       of life

                    a poem

                      barely touches

                       KR Friel

DECEMBER 4

    Willana Bonner was not content to let our ERA
argument just stop so she spent several weeks doing
research and wrote this paper which she read to the
class.

                  Equal Rights Amendment
                  by Willana Marie Bonner

    For decades American women have been
fighting for full personhood. Today, the woman
of today continues this struggle and,
ironically, before she herself has won full
status, she faces yet another obstacle—the
controversy as to whether the unborn fetus is
endowed with the rights of ''personhood'', and
whether she should be forced to acknowledge its
rights above her own. This dilemma is very much
in keeping with her history. Under English

Common law an unmarried woman was first subject
to her father, or brother, and after marriage
she became subject to her husband and sons.
Today, she is being threatened with the
possibility of becoming subject to an unborn
fetus.

On January 22, 1973, when the Supreme Court
ruled that it was unconstitutional to prohibit
women from obtaining abortions, the bitter
struggle appeared to have ended. Unfortunately,
that was not the case. Since the ruling, anti-
choice advocates who claim to be concerned about
life have been working diligently to strike it
down by petitioning the Judicial system to pass
an anti-abortion amendment to the Constitution.
The first signs of legal erosion began in
December 1977 when the Supreme Court ruled that,
''It is not sex discrimination within the
meaning of Title VII of the 1964 Civil Rights
Act to treat pregnancy and related disabilities,
or exclude them from coverage entirely, in
employee insurance plans.'' This was a result of
court action General Electric versus Gilbert.

The second blow was more dramatic. On June
20, 1977 the U.S. Supreme Court held by six to
three that neither Title XIX (Medicaid) of the
Social Security Act nor the Constitution
requires that states pay Medicaid benefits for
abortions which are not ''medically necessary,''
and that public hospitals do not have to provide
abortion services.

On August 4, 1977 the federal government
issued a death blow to indigent women and
stopped paying for abortions for the poor unless
the ''life of the mother was endangered.'' The
first known death as a result of the cutoff came
to a 27 year old Mexican-American woman, the
unwed mother of a four-year-old, in McAllen,
Texas. The young woman died as a result of
massive complications sustained during the
performance of a $40 back alley abortion in a
Mexican border town after she was refused a

federally funded legal abortion. The Federal
Center for Disease Control also confirmed that
four other women had been treated for
complication from Mexican abortions at the same
hospital—one reportedly requiring $ 10,000 worth
of corrective surgery.

After months of battle in Congress (between
the Senate and the House of Representatives over
the language of the bill) a so-called
liberalized version of the 1976 Hyde Amendment
passed. It allows Medicaid recipients to obtain
an abortion only under the following conditions:
1. certification by one physician that
continuation of a pregnancy may endanger the
life of the mother; 2. certification by two
physicians that continuing of a pregnancy may
cause ''severe and longlasting physical damage''
to the woman; 3. such medical procedures
necessary for the victims of rape or incest (to
be reported within 60 days.)

This law is having a profound effect on the
poor and under its restrictions, few Medicaid
recipients are eligible for a legal abortion.
Indignant women are now coerced into a number of
negative options: 1. to allow the fetus to come
to term against their will; 2. to seek an
illegal abortion or; 3. to perform a self-
induced coat-hangar abortion. Women would,
however, be in serious error if we imagine that
this victimization is of concern solely to the
poor. As long as some women's civil and human
rights are restricted, the rights of all women
are endangered. This does not involve only
families on Welfare. Contrary to popular belief,
Welfare recipients do not constitute the
majority of the poor. The fact is that,
according to the Social Security Administration,
there is approximately 5.3 million indigent
women of child-bearing age in America, and of
these only 14% are eligible for Medicaid. This
leaves more than 4 million women virtually
without adequate medical care, including
abortion.

The recent passage of the antiabortion amendment now threatens the hard-earned achievements made so far. Since the 1973 Supreme Court decision removing abortion from the criminal law code, abortion-linked deaths and injuries due to illegal abortions have declined dramatically, and medically safe procedures have largely replaced back-alley butchershop practices. Thousands of women and their families have been relieved of the economic and social hardships of unacceptable pregnancies. There is enough evidence to show that a state can remain viable only if there is a high concern for the life of its children. It is in this spirit that the international Year of the Child 1979 has declared one of its primary goals: ''Every child a wanted one!''

The controversy over the right to abortion has reached such high emotional levels that debates frequently end in a cry that ''Either you're for killing babies, or you're against killing babies!'' Abortion rights have become so embroiled in questions of law, ethics, religion, and morals, that we lose sight of its primary concern which is that abortion is a public health problem—it is a medical service sought by thousands of women who face undesired pregnancies. To withhold this service does not solve the problem. Forcing women to give birth against their will only serves to break down their health and well being, as well as those of their families and communities.

The crucial point that is lost in the maze of emotional controversy over abortion is the fact that a woman who decides to have an abortion will generally obtain one regardless of whether abortion is legal or not. The Federal government can declare abortion illegal—but, it cannot stop women from obtaining abortions. In view of this reality, the criminalization of abortion merely exposes women to mutilations at the hands of unscrupulous illegal abortionists.

It has been calculated by some that during the mid- 1960's several thousand deaths and as many as 100,000 injuries resulted annually from illegal abortions each year. While current statistics indicate that more than one million legal abortions are now being performed annually, the rate of emergency room complications that have previously resulted from illegal abortions prior to 1973 has declined sharply. Abortion Surveillance: 1974 estimated that maternal deaths related to legally induced abortions were 3. 1 per 100,000-less than that in childbirth.

Antiabortion activists, whose heavy lobbying helped the passage of the antiabortion amendment, include religious groups and organizations such as the Roman Catholic bishops of the U.S. and the National Right to Life Committee. Passage of this amendment represents only a first step in the goal of anti-choice advocates; they have no intention of stopping there. Opponents of abortions intend to stop only when they succeed in outlawing all abortions for all women.

The National Right to Life Committee is one of the most vocal and militant antichoice organizations. Members show a passionate concern for the unborn fetus, but extremely little concern for the total life cycle. A favorite scare tactic is to show color photos of fetuses in the process of being aborted, on the grounds that this has great shock value. However, they fail to show photos of women who are left to die of hemorrhages from illegal abortionists—a situation with equal shock value. Their position negatively links abortion with crimes of war, euthanasia child experimentation and genocide.

Should women become tempted to sympathize with this brand of concern for life, we have only to note that, due to heavy pressure from antiabortionists, the March of Dimes is now phasing out its current support of established

genetics centers that can diagnose major birth
defects before birth, called amniocentesis,
which included Down's syndrome (mongolism), Tay-
Sachs disease and sickle cell anemia. Right to
Life members do not believe that women have the
right to decide if they want a deformed fetus to
come to term. The irony is that in their craze
to save fetuses, they overlook the fact that
according to the geneticist, Dr. Aubrey Milunsky
of Harvard Medical School, ''far more babies
have been born because of amniocentesis to women
who otherwise would never have dared become
pregnant for fear of some defect that ran in
their families than those not born because of
abortion.''

More tragically, Jimmy Carter has allowed
his personal anti-abortion views to influence
his presidential responsibilities. Carter's now
famous statement, ''life is unfair'' shocked the
nation when he expressed the view that ''there
are many things in life that are not fair, that
wealthy people can afford and poor people can't—
the federal government should not take action to
try to make these opportunities exactly equal,
particularly, when there is a moral factor
involved.'' This is strictly Carter's own
interpretation of what constitutes Federal
government responsibility. Although there is no
doubt that the rich can afford superior medical
care than the poor, the Federal government is
indeed responsible since it is deeply involved
in the medical services of millions of indigent
people. This is the same president who says he
is concerned with human rights around the world,
while American women are deprived of
reproduction freedom.

Joseph A. Califano, Secretary of the
Department of Health, Education, and Welfare, is
in accord with Carter's views. He made it clear
that ''whether discriminatory or not, his
policies at HEW would be, to the extent possible
under the law, to make sure that no federal
funds are used for Medicaid abortions.''

The appropriation of federal funds to provide abortion services has become a convenient handle for those who are opposed to offering women a choice of abortion. As callous as the federal government and some members of Congress often appear, it is difficult to believe that their attempt to regulate abortion is influenced in terms of monetary value alone. The ethical cost/benefit of abortion can be measured only in terms of the health and welfare of women versus human suffering. Antiabortion advocates, however, find it more to their advantage to exploit the poor by using economics and racism to incite them against exercising their right to choice. Antiabortionists contend that abortion is a ''crime against the poor,'' (especially Black women.) Antiabortionists claim that it is in the interest of white society to discourage Black women from having children since the Federal government saves millions in Welfare costs.

This cloaked concern for the ''rights of the Black women'' is highly questionable, not only because their premise is primarily based on the perpetuation of racial dissension, but because, while they appear to give Black women ''a right to bear children,'' on one hand, they take away the ''right of choice'' with the other. They neglect to inform us that prior to 1973, when abortion was a crime, 85% of the women who died as a result of illegal abortions were Black and brown women. Antichoice advocates glibly label abortion for the poor as ''genocide'' and use the strategy of confusing the terms force with choice. The fact is genocide is a deliberate and systematic act of annihilation. The legalization of abortion merely offers a choice.

Abortion is by no means a solution to poverty. No responsible person would advocate abortion as a means of birth control. In a society where contraception is far from perfect, or not easily attainable for many, abortion merely serves as a back-up when methods of prevention fail. Abortion is not a crime against the poor; the crime is when society first subjects a segment of its people to economic deprivation, then scorns them for their dependence on public funds for their survival and health care.

This discrimination is not only against welfare recipients, but also pregnant young adolescents. The rising number of pregnancies among adolescents is a growing concern. It is estimated that 1.5 million young people in America are sexually active; of the total number of women who opt for abortion, one-third are teenagers. Prevention of unwanted pregnancies should be the primary goal. There is a need for a clearer understanding both from the family and the professional in regard to sexuality among adolescents. It can no longer be denied that young people are in need of sex education, contraception information, and counseling. Contraceptive devices should be made easily accessible to youngsters without creation of an atmosphere of fear or embarrassment.

Adolescents who are already pregnant, and who wish to have the child, need health and mental counseling, nutritional services, parenting education and, there is a critical need for nursery and day care centers to enable the teenager to continue her schooling, or to seek employment. Adoption is an especially traumatic experience for the teenager who decides to give up the child and she should be provided with emotional support and professional counseling. For those young people who choose not to have the child, guidance, and provisions must be made available for a safe and legal abortion.

The moral issue of abortion is perhaps the most controversial of all. Morality has been closely linked with the question of what constitutes human life, that is at what point does life begin—at conception, or at birth? And does the destruction of the fetus constitute the

taking of a life? Until now it has been
virtually impossible for the Supreme Court
ruling (removing abortion from the criminal
code) and the 1977 amendment, seem to indicate a
rejection of the idea that life and personhood
begin at the moment of conception and implies
that termination of the fetus is not considered
murder.

Morality cannot be legislated as we learned
by the total failure of the 18th Amendment which
made Prohibition the law of the land and
stimulated more immoral acts than it curbed.
There are millions of thoughtful conscientious
and religious people, including the Religious
Coalition for Abortion Rights (RCAR), who
believe that it's immoral to bear a child that
one can't care fore lovingly and responsibly and
that abortion can be a painful but deeply moral
choice. In matters of human reproduction the
right of choice reflects true justice since one
need not choose abortion for oneself to be in
favor of its availability to others.

A further erosion of existing abortion laws,
not targeted to the poor, is in serious jeopardy
of spreading to all women. If it isn't brought
to a hault, a return of abortion to the criminal
law code will mean a return to the horrendous
health conditions that existed prior to the 1973
Supreme Court ruling. The right to safe health
care is a human right that belongs to all women,
and protection of these rights can't be left in
the hands of those who seek to deny women, and
their families, the opportunity to determine how
they will shape their lives.

DECEMBER 5

Butch Wade's final journal entry of the
semester.

Corine

The person who I am writing about is a lady.
The most important lady in my life today, my
grandmother. This woman is six foot four and has
a very dark complexion, and bowlegged. She was
born in the country in Tennessee. Her name is
Corine! Corine Kennedy. Looking back into the
past I can remember when I was about twelve,
Corine told me to go outside and get a switch,
which to me was a small branch of a tree or a
twig of a bush. I would come back with the
switch, crying and begging for mercy all the
while. ''Go lay over the chair'' Corine would
say. Every time at that exact moment I would
always make a run for the door and she would
catch me before I opened the door and whipped me
harder for runing. Well this time I left the
door open and ran through the door and down the
street. I ran to the park and hid in a play
tunnel. I stayed in the tunnel all night, to
afraid to come home. The next morning I ran home
and went into the kitchen where she was sitting.
''I'm sorry, Corine, were you worried about
me?'' I said. She looked at me with tears in her
eyes and said ''Yes, I cried all night'' and
gave me a big hug. I was so happy to be wanted.
She made me breakfast and when I finished eating
she frowned and said ''Now go get me another
switch boy.'' And I did. I remember that
experience with alot of joy. Later in my life
when I was sixteen I had become what she termed
as a antique punk or a thug. I had produced a
child, gotten kicked out of numerous schools,
rolled, mugged and whatever else for money. One
day while walking with my gang, Lance, the
leader said ''Let's take that lady's purse,''
everyone agreed. Just before the lady approach
us I said ''Wait. That's my grandmother.'' When
she walked past she grabbed me by my afro and
said ''You were going to snitch my purse werent
you.'' No, I said, But she continued to grasp my
hair until we had gotten home. She said ''You

will graduate next month and I think ya should
join the service. You are always into no good
and one day ya will be killed.'' ''If I go into
the service I will probably be killed,'' I
screamed. She started crying, and it was the
first time I had ever seen her cry since her
husband died 10 years ago. So like the fool I
was I went and joined the Navy two days later. I
had 30 days before graduation and 66 days before
I had to enter the service. And every night
after that I would go pick her up from work at
12 and we would sit and talk until 2 or 3.
Finally when I went into boot camp, which is the
first training stage in the military, I found
that many of the girls, guys and family had
cease to write, but Corine would write twice a
week as she said she would and during all the
humiliation, and frustration that occured, I
knew I would have went AWOL or left the camp if
it wasn't for Corine. That is my Corine and I
hope I have shown her to you.

Chapter XXI

Go to the cafeteria and really concentrate on the multiplicity of events. Think of the stories behind each person. Try to be aware of as many different parts of the room as you can. Think of the materials, the small pieces of stone and paper and wood that are around you. Where did they come from—Wisconsin? Utah? Georgia? How many people have had contact with all these little parts? Notice the colors—what makes them up? Listen to the sound—what goes into making them? Then contemplate what it took to bring all these cells and vibrations together at this one moment.

Another activity: Write a review of all the things you've done today. Simply jot down all that has happened to you or around you today. Record everything you've done and as much as you can remember that you've thought. Don't ignore anything. Get it all down.

Is it any wonder that we feel overwhelmed from time to time, that we want somehow for there to be some sense to be made from all this madness? That we want some order out of all this chaos?

A couple of years ago I got the following letter from my son Larry and I saved it. It shows him trying at a very early age (eight years old then), trying to organize his universe into some kind of sensible pattern using words to do it.

Dear Dad,

I am doing good in school. The best class in school is reading. I have 15 book reports. A lot better than last year isn't it. The Chi Bears won their first game 2 weeks ago aginst Pitt. 38 to 7. But their still not doing very hot. They got beat 48–31 just this Sunday. My football shoes are just fine. One night I went outside with my football shoes on and kicked my football. But I got a blister and couldn't play in them for a while.

Love

Larry

First, notice the obvious three-part division of the letter, one part about school, next the Bears, and finally his own career in football. That kind of dividing up and ordering is obvious. But notice also how the words function as labels for categories and help him make some sense out of an infinite number of things in his mind: "good," "better than last year," "fine." But most important is to realize that each label makes use of categories which include some things and exclude everything else. For example, "school" includes one part of his life and excludes everything else. "Class" does the same and "reading" narrows the category even further. "Play" refers to a category of actions. Even words like "with," "and," and "than" refer to categories.

In short, throughout the piece, we see an eight-year-old boy dealing with his universe, separating it into parts, labeling those parts and using language to do it. We see him separating his life into categories: "got beat" (not "won"). "Bears" (not "Lions" or "Bengals" or "Raiders")., "blister" (not "sore" or "scratch" or "pain"), and "on" (not "off").

 Discuss: All the stuff in life that the letter organizes, all the moments that it took to make school "good." Also think of the stuff he excludes: the friends, games he played, cuts and bruises, "bad" moments in school, and so on. See how the letter orders his existence?

The next piece is very similar. It's something David Kuester wrote. When I read it, it reminded me of Larry's letter. Again, it's a beautiful recording of a human trying to make sense of a chaotic world.

On the face of it, David seems to be writing to you about me. But he's really doing what Larry did—only in this case, it's an adult who is less satisfied with a simple picture made of simple parts. David sees more complications, more relationships, and he knows he's got a good bit of ice underwater, which he had to expose if the piece is to express himself.

When you read it, you should sense the good-humored struggle David is having while he tries to make sense of his vision of one part of his universe—his perceptions of me. Notice how he seems from time to time simply to give up on order and to accept ideas, perceptions as they come. But, of course, it's impossible to *reproduce* the chaos that his world—or yours or mine or anybody else's, for that matter—is. Just the act of writing, because of the categorizing nature of words, gives order to the universe. You might want to think about that as you read it—language is an ordering device. Not only *can* we use language to order the universe; but when we use language, we are forced to order the universe because ordering is what language does.

The things that most people notice about Dick first are his beard and the way he dresses. We stop and think, because in both of these ways he is out of the ordinary, and when we see something novel or new, that's a natural reaction.

He doesn't dress with much respect for what others like to see, but rather to express something of himself, to impose part of himself on himself, to present a certain picture to the outside world that comes from within.

A picture of Dick on a given day might have a lot to do with beards and beads, or a gigantic glass medallion that looks like it came from an elegant chandelier, or a white shirt with a Nehru collar and sleeves that get fuller and more flowing as they get longer. It might have to do with a pair of cowboy boots that he paid one hundred and fifty bucks for and will continue to pay for over the next six months. Or it might even have to do with a brown suit, and a rather bland necktie.

When Dick wears a bland necktie, you can bet that if you look long enough and hard enough, you'll find something a little offbeat about the rest of what he's wearing. At his wedding, he showed up with a brown suit, pin-striped shirt, and bland necktie. He was wearing, in the lapel of his coat, the most outrageous boutonniere I had ever seen. It was twice as big as most boutonnieres and three times as big as it should have been.

He surprised everyone who attended the wedding ceremony by wearing that conservative suit, but the boutonniere didn't surprise anyone, and I looked down at his feet, half-expecting to see the cowboy boots he had bought the day before.

There's no telling if he will show up for his own wedding in a conservative brown suit or dressed like his own version of a hippie. There's no telling whether he will be wearing plain brown shoes or cowboy boots.

So I don't try to predict any more. I just sit back—as I suppose he does from time to time—and enjoy being a little amused.

And I'm sure that the way he starts off a day is by asking himself: How do I feel? What should I wear today? What kind of mood am I in? Should I entertain my students? Blow their minds? Fit their image of what a teacher should look like? Challenge the whole code?

That's the way I imagine him in the morning, going through the ritual of asking himself how he feels that day and what kind of impression he wants to make on those he encounters.

I remember the first English Department party.

I had worn a double-breasted blue blazer and white turtleneck sweater, and I felt I had really broken the mold, because no one there had ever seen me out of my uniform of a suit and tie.

So I felt a little self-conscious, and, I admit, rather dashing and debonaire.

And then I saw Friedrich.

I saw him and I wondered if he had actually driven over there in his car, and wondered if he had stopped at a filling station to get gas, and actually talked to the guys who fill up your gas tank dressed like that.

He was all in white. Like Colonel Sanders. Only more so.

He was wearing white slacks and white socks and white suede shoes, and a white shirt that had been made for him by some avant-garde tailor in Los Angeles.

And around his neck hung the most outrageous piece of masculine jewelry I had ever seen. It was the medallion, a massive piece of big and little chunks of oblong and circular crystal, taken, I think, from the last foot of a massive chandelier in a Victorian whorehouse. And it was bright blue.

And people were gathering around him and just staring, and he knew them all so it wasn't too bad, and he was laughing and enjoying it all, and I stood there, in the corner, in my blue blazer, thinking that next time I might even wear a blue turtleneck and a peace symbol.

What's happened today is that the rebels in our society have broken through old styles and substituted new ones. America has absorbed the styles and substituted new ones. America has absorbed the styles of the dissenters into the mainstream of its life. But the real test of the strength—the test of the true individualism—of any society is whether it can not only absorb new trends, but respect and admire those few who don't fit any trend, don't follow any leaders.

They are the ones who don't care what the guy in the filling station says, or who care less about that than about their own freedom and individuality.

 Remember the list you made of all the events, ideas, and perceptions that came to you in one day? Use that list to write an account of that day; see how writing about the day unavoidably orders it; writing about it may even give some sense of logic to the day that you weren't aware of before. After everybody has finished writing, share some with the rest of the class—have a few writers read their papers to the class. Discuss the act of writing as an act which orders—no matter what you do, you order things when you use language. Of course, since you can't avoid using language, you have to relate to the universe as having order. Maybe it doesn't? Are you even free to think of nature as chaotic? Are you thus a slave to language?

Another activity: Choose one object or person from that same day and write about it as completely as you can: try to show what that object "meant" to you. Did it remind you of something? Did it make you realize anything new? Did it stir any thoughts in you? After you've finished, divide into groups of three or four and read each others' papers. Then discuss.

From the time we hear our first "no, no" until they lower our bodies into the earth in exact keeping with the law—both written and unwritten—our lives are guided (controlled?) by categories. Some acts are labeled "Just not done," like sleeping in church, men wearing dresses, and questioning teachers. Other acts are labeled "wrong" or "immoral," like killing another human (unless in the category of "condemned" or "guilty" or "enemy"). Other acts are "illegal": driving faster than the limit and fishing without a license are examples of that. Most of these categories are set up without our consent—I had nothing to do with the development of men's and women's fashions, nor with deciding which "enemies" of "my" country could be killed. In fact I had nothing to do with deciding who are "allies" and who are "enemies." So writing those rules is pretty much beyond my control; of course, I can always decide to obey or disobey them.

Those sets of do and don't categories agreed upon by a group of people are another kind of rule. People sit down together and try to decide what categories of actions they will agree to perform.

But no matter whether a rule is declared with my consent and participation or totally without them, it's still a word problem. That is laws are not a part of our nature the way eating or sleeping or dying are. Those activities are carried on (or can be) entirely without the aid of words. And they are completely beyond human control—we have to eat, we have to die. (Some call these "laws of nature" as though nature made "laws.") A speed limit is not the same thing as a "law of nature," nor are the laws of personal property, nor is the injunction against killing. All these laws are made with languages and by humans who can change them if they want. (Or can they?)

 At any rate, since we do not ordinarily think of rule writing as merely a word game, let's have some experience. Break into groups of five or six and write a constitution—or a contract, agreement, or set of rules for this course. Let each group take one topic (grading, attendance, procedures), then come back together as a whole class to agree on a final constitution (or whatever) for the rest of the semester. Decide what the course should deal with. Also how. What about being disruptive? What use will your class make of the instructor? And who's going to be the "instructor" anyway?

DECEMBER 6

And Gary Jostes's last journal entry.

English Comp. I has been an interesting
course for me. The desire to express myself in
writing has always been strong. Although little
time is available for developing writing skills,
this course made it necessary for me to
practice. As we all know, practice is the only
route to perfection.
During the course of the semester, new ideas
and concepts I would never have given
consideration, were introduced. I hope that some
of my thoughts and comments were considered by
others. I know I have watched and learned from
all involved.
Perhaps more could have been taught in the
classroom, but I doubt it. It seems the greatest
strides were made on a personal basis; the
transition of ideas to our journals.

DECEMBER 8

Willy liked the idea of writing a children's
story so much that he wrote one for his own kids for
Christmas and included it in his journal here.

Christmas with Santa

Willy Jr. and Shelley were both looking out
of the living room window waiting for Nana.
Kermit was laying on the floor by the door where
he usually lays. He knew something special was
going to happen because both Willy and Shelley
were so excited all day.
It was Christmas Eve and the snow was so
deep outside that the Pontiac was almost covered
with snow—only the roof was sticking out. Just
then the phone rang and you could tell by the
way mom's voice sounded that something was

wrong. She came into the living room and told
Willy and Shelley that there was so much snow at
the airport that the airplanes couldn't land.
Nana would not be able to fly in from Arizona to
be with them.

The rest of the day went by very slow and
Willy and Shelley were very unhappy. That night
mom and dad tucked them in bed and told them
that it would be alright. ''We can all still
have Christmas without Nana'' said dad. ''It
won't be much fun'' pouted Willy. ''No fun at
all,'' said Shelley.

Late that night Santa landed on the roof to
delivery Willy and Shelley's presents. When he
came down the Chimney he heard Shelley crying so
he walked up the steps and snuck into her room
and said, ''Ho-Ho-Ho, why are you crying
Shelley.'' ''Nana won't be with us on
Christmas,'' Shelley told him. ''Let's wake up
your brother and go down stairs so we don't wake
up your mom and dad,'' whispered Santa.

They went downstairs and Santa told them to
put their coats on and not to worry.

Then Santa got into the fireplace and said
''Follow me.'' He touched his finger on his nose
and away he went.

Shelley was afraid so Willy took her hand
and said ''Come on Shelley—it will be O.K.—Santa
said so.'' They touched their fingers on their
noses and like magic up the fireplace they flew.
When they came out of the top of the fireplace
on the roof they landed right in Santa's sleigh.
And there was the eight reindeer led by Rudolph
with his nose glowing red.

''Don't worry,'' said Santa''—my reindeer
can go where airplanes can't.'' Away they went
higher than the clouds and Willy and Shelley
were having so much fun. It didn't take long
before they got to Nana's house. Nana doesn't
have a fireplace so they landed in the driveway.
Willy and Shelley ran to the front door and rang
the doorbell. Nana came to the door with her two

dogs Bridgette and Finese. She was so happy and
excited. ''Come on Nana Santa is taking us to
our house,'' said Shelley. So Nana, Willy and
Shelley, Santa, Bridgette, and Finese all got
into Santa's sleigh and away they went. It
didn't take long before they were back at home
again. This time Santa left them off in the
street. Willy and Shelley told Santa thanks and
gave him a big hug and a kiss. Santa told
Rudolph, ''Away Rudolph—let's deliver the
presents,'' and away they flew. ''Merry
Christmas to All,'' said Santa as they flew over
the house. Willy and Shelley took Nana by the
hands and they went in the house to tell mom and
dad all about their wonderful trip in Santa's
sleigh.

DECEMBER 11

We seem to have come full circle. I started this
journal explaining my nervousness about the first
day of class and, here, I finish it about to explain
my nervousness on the last day of class. Did I do
the things I wanted to do? Did I fail to cover some
important ideas?
I suppose, if I'm honest, I know that this
semester is like many others for me. I start out
with big plans about what I'm going to ''teach'' and
wind up fascinated by what my students write,
forgetting to teach as I remember that I'm much more
interested in learning. In my learning about myself
and my students, in my learning along with my
students more about language and communication as we
sruggle to make sense to each other.
I notice as I look back through this journal
that it became more and more the class's journal and
less and less the teacher's journal. And I guess
that I am pleased about that. My words alone could
not explain this semester as it is explained here by
the students as they wrote their way through it.

So I thank them all —

    William

    Trudy

    Ray

    Arran

    Joice

    Brenda

    Loretta

    Kevin

    Gary

    Paul

    Richard

    Fran

    Clare

    Pat

    Butch

    Tanya

    Rosie

    Willy

    Ralph

    Carol

    Sara

    Walt

    Don

    Judy

I thought the semester was over but I was wrong
again. Don Hensley came by my office today and with
a sort of funny smile asked me if I remembered
Dick's brown leather arm chair. We both knew that
his question didn't require an answer so he handed
me these pieces and said, ''Here's mine.''

So I read them and told him I wished that I'd
written or done them (I'm not quite sure what verb
applies) and I meant it.

Here are Don's last two pieces:

1367
munching apples
juice pours into
the next day
filling
the pores
and grooves
that were
abandoned
so long ago
by conquistadors
gold hungry bellies
cloaked in iron —
cross held up high
marching eternal march
fierce and unafraid . . .
"they've come from across the waters"
—look who sickens
at the sight of human sacrifice!
Montezuma feared his gods
mistaking Cortez "the righteous killer"
as god in vengence
then stoned to death by his people
(act of god in vengence)
c i v i l i z a t i o n ravaged
by a handful of starving spaniards
—they came for gold
but stole the very existence
of the Indian empire

Don Hensley

red pen ink
red strike two edged sword
fugitive gold in milk dust
loose tassles wiggle generous
shifting eyes search down,

stained petite pin-stripe shadows
without edges
raw tongue laps up tightly
around chin

stretching fingers dig,
scratch beneath numb nails
taste sharp, warm bristled beard
slime-blue viscous goo spreads
cautious over even tanned limb,
where brilliant white shore sparkles flash
"like colour slides in a circle spectrum"
revolving around dark brooding gushes
of echoed air waves drooling over—

freshly exposed meat
yesterdays ego cascades freely
curiously bouncing
out the kitchen faucet
off stainless sink,
shattering keen-edged
ping thru muddy hearing
escaping my fresh senses
instantly minds sucked themselves
inside out
flop!

long enough to moisten dried out
memories fading at whim
hopelessy obscuring
all details from
recognition

Don Hensley

Meditations

So here we are, poor innocents wandering through our lives, looking to our language to help us order our chaotic universe and the language not only lets us down, but it makes us think it hasn't. It lies to us about itself, it seems to define the world by dividing it into neat, separate categories when all it's doing is approximating reality.

Discuss: What we find in language is that the categories don't really exist anywhere but in our minds—all these words seem to refer to things when they're really not—or are they? Or are "referring to things" and "not referring to things"—just another pair of categories that don't quite hold up the way we want them to?

What I've been saying is that from one point of view, language is a device which we use to cope with three horrors of our existence: (1) our mortality—the constant change and our share of that change; (2) our loneliness, and (3) the chaos which we perceive our universe to be. I've tried to communicate that language as a tool in this struggle is less than satisfactory. In fact, at times, it's not even "better than nothing." (Think about that phrase for a while.) So what do we do? If language doesn't work very well as a way of meeting reality, why not desert it?

My theory is that humanity is evolving new devices to solve these three problems. By evolving, I do not mean that there is some kind of pattern or plan. I mean that as time goes on, individuals are learning and passing on different (not necessarily better) devices to cope with and understand reality. Perhaps, as we pass on our devices from generation to generation, our descendants will survive. Perhaps word language will disappear over the centuries. And perhaps humans will disappear. But before I get us off too far into the realm of the unreal future, I should get on to my own life and how I deal with language.

Even though I know language is unsatisfactory, and even though I know how unsatisfactory it is, I'm stuck with it. For now language is an integral part of my own struggle to live and remain sane. The notions of my own impermanence, the impermanence of the universe, my aloneness, and the chaos of my universe are unbearable to my stomach, but I perceive them in my mind. I'm "certain" they are accurate perceptions, and I "believe" them.

But even though it is totally inconsistent to live in defiance of the best my mind can tell me, I do not base my life on my mental perceptions. Instead I go about the business of life as though I assume that these perceptions are faulty (even though I *think* they are not), and that through language I do relate accurately to the universe around me and the other humans in that universe. And as really optimistic as this might seem, I think that communication does happen from time to time. So here I sit writing.

There's one more area of difficulty about the relationship of my language and my world and the way I see my world. Simply stated, the questions are these: Does my language label the universe more or less as it is or does my language actually control my perception of that universe? Do my language's categories reflect (roughly) nature and thus provide me with a systematic, though imperfect, device for dealing with reality? Or does my language force me to see my universe in a way that separates me from reality? Do I control my vision and use language to describe what I see? Or do I see what I see because of my language? Does my language thus control me?

The problems I tried to define above were defined as difficulties between me and my universe—and language was simply a device to confront the universe. Is it possible that the real struggle is not between me and the universe? Could it be that the real difference is not between my language and my universe? Could it be that the struggle is between me and my language, that the real difference is between the universe and my perception of it? The green that I see? Is it really there the way I see it? Or do I see it because I speak English?

I'll tell you what I think right now—I think that I see the world not the way it is—but the way my language limits me to seeing it.

Let's go back to the color spectrum. Are there actually separate colors like blue, green, and yellow? I see them. I can put my finger on the green part of the spectrum and on the yellow. But then remember again how I learned the color: whole bunches of objects connected for me by the sound "yellow," others connected for me by the sound "green." Finally, concepts emerged in my head which I labeled "yellow and "green." Then when I came to the color spectrum in school one day, sure enough—there they were. In between them was an area which we could call—let's see, it's a combination of yellow and green—let's call it "yellow-green."

But what if I was born and raised in Rhodesia and spoke Shona?

Here's what linguists tell me I'd see. Instead of seeing this part in between yellow and green as a combination of two colors, I'd see a color—a pure color—which I'd call "cicena." You'd want me to understand "orange" as a color and I'd be seeing a lighter part of one color called "cipswuka": which would include what you call "red." Now maybe what you call "yellow" I'd call "light cicena," and what you call "red" I'd call "dark cipswuka," but I'd still see what you call "red" and what you call "orange" as two parts of one color—just as you see "bright yellow" and "deep yellow" as two parts of one color. And what you see as "yellow" and what you see as "green," I'd see as one color—just one dark and the other light. And what you see as a wishy-washy combination of two colors and call "yellow-green," I'd see as the most intense part of a color called "cicena."*

Since we've (most of us) never spoken Shona, we probably never before considered that there are other ways of dissecting the color spectrum. No, the reason we say "green" and "yellow" and "orange" was simply that they were there. We continue to see them because they continue to be there. Our language has seemed to be a way of labeling nature *the way it is*; it never occurs to us that we see nature the way we see it because our language forces us to.

There are, we think, words like "snow," "rain," "clouds," "purple," "running," "falling," "in," "out," "now" and "then" because what these words stand for is out there in nature and we need words to stand for it. So we (or somebody or somebodies) got the words.

It goes like this: we see the world, then we see the parts of it, then we name those parts. Sort of like Adam. Or at least we learn from somebody what to call these parts of nature. Like being Adam's kids.

But look at it this way. I, as a small child, see the world as an infinite series of objects. Then, along come the adults of my language group. They pass their language on to me—with its categories, its own ways of dissecting and organizing the world. From time to time I learn my colors. I see the color spectrum divided the way my language divides it. That's what "learning my colors" means.

But I'll tend to assume that the way I see the world is the way the world really is. My language shapes my vision so thoroughly that I come to think that it reflects nature—that the reason there is a word "snow" is that there is a category of nature to correspond to the word.

However, nature is still as it was when I was a baby: an infinite series of stuff, a whole big mass—just like the color spectrum. What has happened is in me: I have come to categorize nature according to the lines laid down by my language.

Here's another way of approaching the same basic problem of having reality dissected for us and then thinking that's the way nature is. Take the notes in music. Sounds are divided into C, C#, D, D#, E, F, F#, G, G#, A, A#, B. Seven notes and five half-notes—twelve steps, sort of evenly spaced out. Right? Almost. The fact is that our culture breaks sounds into that set of categories. Other cultures do it quite differently. Ever hear music from another culture? Navajo? Chinese? Part of the reason it sounds so different is that these scales divide the sound spectrum differently from the way ours does. I remember when I was a child, I wondered what goes on *in between* the

*H.A. Gleason, Jr., *An Introduction to Descriptive Linguistics*, rev. ed. (New York: Holt, Rinehart & Winston, 1961).

keys on the piano. Well, I knew that a slide trombone had "real" notes (like the piano's notes), but it also had the sounds *between* those notes. Then I found out even more about these "in between" sounds when I heard my first John Cage music. If you want to know exactly what I mean, check out a tape or record of Cage's music. Or Oriental or Native American music.

That kind of music sounds "wrong" it's not the way "music" is. Last week, I went to the symphony here in St. Louis. We heard a composition which didn't use the regular notes and instruments. The people in the audience kept saying "That's not music." In a way they were accurate—that wasn't the way the sound labeled "music" had been divided up for them previously. In another way they were inaccurate—the way they had had sound divided up for them wasn't the only way to do it.

In fact, even dividing sound into separate notes wasn't the only way to do it, either. What I mean is that a person could look at the whole range of sounds as a big slur and at notes as artificially separated from the big slur. It all depends on how you look at it. And how you look at it (whatever "it" may be) depends, to a large degree, on how the language you are born to divides up nature.

Again the problem is that we tend to think that the way we divide the universe up reflects nature when sometimes it doesn't. Our languages in the Western world use a thing-word for "heat." (I can't say it any other way.) That is, the languages put this aspect of the universe into the category usually reserved for objects, for things. "Dog," "bottle," "word," "heat." As a result, it was a good many years until scientists came to realize that heat is not a thing or a quality, but an action or a degree of motion or something else. (Yes, I'm aware that I said "something," I'm trapped by my language.) They were looking for the substance which was "heat." Just the fact that I have to ask the question this way—"What is heat?"—indicates the way our language tends to see the universe as a series of finite and discrete objects.

Our language has made us see it that way. Maybe the universe is not at all divided. Maybe it isn't objects. What about "sky"? Sit and contemplate what "sky" refers to. Is it an object? A thing? Is it a going on? Does it be?

 Discuss: Are these questions themselves false? In other words, is it just the language that makes it possible to ask such questions? How about lightning? Waves? Icebergs? Tables? Me? Music? Color? Love? A bar of soap? Democracy?

Discuss: Get outside and look at the sky, smog, fog, or rain. What are these things? Are they things? Events? Processes? All of those and more? None of those and less? What is "light"? "Dark"?

236

Finally there are far more questions than answers. I wonder where you are in your semester right now. Maybe you won't have time to discuss all of this in class. Maybe none of it. That's O.K. It's probably better because maybe your semester of English—like your understanding of "sky"—will no longer be a finite thing but a lifelong process, struggle, passion, and part of you. It's nice to think that right now you may be reading this after your "semester" period is done. And maybe you've signed up at a college like the one I've signed up at. It's in my insides; it's part of me and has no requirements, no grades, no teachers vs. students, no administrators, no semesters, no buildings. It's wherever I am at the time and it meets whenever I'm learning or enjoying. There are no classes—only activities and long moments of silence when you can just plain think. And it's free.

Our language (and therefore we) divide reality into sets of two, such as:

(1) Tall and short; fat and skinny; young and old. That's kind of like the wrist-forearm problem, isn't it?

(2) Good and bad. Was Jimmy Carter a "good" President? Is a Shakespeare a "good" playwright? Does Ford make "good" cars? Are you living a "good" life? Is it "good" to eat foods like butter which are "bad" for you? If so, how "good"?

(3) Beautiful and ugly. How many human beings have had their lives shaped by this dubious set of categories? Is this pair like the tall-short pair? Or is it like the good-bad pair? Or is it like neither?

(4) Guilty and innocent. What does it mean to say a man is "guilty"? Consider the accidents—the elements beyond his control—that make it impossible for a guy to do something. Think: a murder needs somebody who will get killed, somebody who will kill, the means to achieve the killing, the killer in the right mood (just think of all the contributing factors there), and besides, how many times have you and I been capable of killing and the situation just wasn't right?

(5) We and they. If a language had only "me," "you," "him," "them," (no "us"), could the people who speak that language wage war? What if it had no *them*?

(6) Smart and stupid. What does it mean to say someone is "smart"? Do you have to be "smarter" to become a doctor or a mechanic—what kind of doctor and what kind of mechanic? Are some skills more important than others—doctor, bricklayer, teacher, poet, clergyman, janitor? Important to whom? Are some skills more difficult than others? Verbal skills? Mechanical? Mathematical? Artistic? Difficult for whom? "Difficult?" "Important?" Is an "A" student "smarter" than an "F" student? Even if, by some quirk of fate, the grade somehow approximates what the student accomplishes in the course? (And as a side note, what would be the effect—if any—of your answer on the school you go to, if they accepted your answer as "true"?)

(7) Yes and no. Some things are and some things aren't. Are some things both? Is that conceivable? If not, does its being inconceivable make it impossible? Or is it possible that the "yes-no" set of mutually exclusinve categories is faulty?

(8) The person who does (or is) something and what s/he does (or is).

Is it possible to see the world where actor and action are not separate at all? We have to say "The lightning flashed," and "The noise exploded," and "The flame burned," As though the lightning, flame, and noise were doing something. But they are object and action together. In "The girl hit the ball," we see the hitting as the connection between the girl and the ball. But it's possible to see the girl and hitting as one unit and the ball as the other. Or the hitting and the ball as one unit and the girl as the other. Or all three as one—not as three separate parts of one, as bricks seem to be separate parts of one wall, but as merging realities making a new reality—as the words, music, voice lose their individual identities to become a new object when they get into my head.

Or what about the idea of cause and effect, the idea that anything, that happens or is, happens or is *because* of something. That is, everything is "caused" somehow. I wonder—is the notion of cause and effect simply a language-induced notion? I wonder if a person can imagine a world-vision in which the distinction between "cause" and "effect" doesn't exist. Are things really "caused" by other things? What does "cause" mean anyway?

We say that in the process of evolution, humans lost their tails because they no longer needed them. Or that whales developed thick layers of blubber to insulate them from the cold water. This sounds like humans and "whales" actually caused something or at least were there when something or at least were there when something was happening to them. Did it work this way? Since there never existed such a creature as "man" or "whale," but only single objects (call them Dick and Moby Dick), how did the process happen in these individual things? We also say "Nature provided chewing teeth for some animals and tearing teeth for others." Who, or what, is Nature? Is it necessary that a cause was involved in who got what kind of teeth?

Could it be that you and I have a hard time seeing a world with all those phenomena and no causes simply because our language, with its pattern of "The guy who does/is—what he does/is," makes us see the world as a place where all things have a cause? Or is the concept of cause-effect in our language because it really exists out there in nature?

Where does all this lead us? To some basic questions about reality, ourselves, and language. The whole book has been based on the notion that "writing" and "writer" are much more a merging of incredibly complicated inseparable elements, than simply a person sitting down and learning how to write. Saying that "you are writing your thoughts in your language," sounds like all we have to do is teach you (1) how to write; (2) how to think clearly; and (3) how language operates in you and others. Then you'll be able to get the job done.

People have been approaching the problem that way for generations. And it's never worked. We've tried to approach you and your ideas and your language and your writing as simply different aspects of the same reality.

We think also that you can come to realize a lot about yourself from looking carefully at that part of you that is referred to as your language.

Well, at any rate, here I am at the end of a book (lines on pages symbolizing concepts in my mind which a reader may or may not understand the way I intend). The book is not only about language, but about how to use it effectively. And also how seeing language helps to see ourselves and how that sight helps us to become writers.

Knowing the limitations of me, and the limitations of me using language to communicate to you, I am amused at our arrogance. In our ignorance and mortality and loneliness, caught in the same chaotic universe. Trying to make some sense out of it and trying to bring our visions together. And then hoping to send it off to you (and we don't know you or even who you are), hoping that some kind of bond of communication may take place.